RIVERSIDE COMMUNITY COLLEGE
1916

P9-DXI-219

DATE DUE

FE 24 98			

Demco, Inc. 38-293

COUNTDOWN!

COUNTDOWN!

FRED KOGER

ALGONQUIN BOOKS OF CHAPEL HILL   1990

Published by
Algonquin Books of Chapel Hill
Post Office Box 2225
Chapel Hill, North Carolina 27515-2225

a division of
Workman Publishing Company, Inc.
708 Broadway
New York, New York 10003

Library of Congress Cataloging-in-Publication Data
Koger, Fred, 1924–
    Countdown! / by Fred Koger.
        p.   cm.
    ISBN 0-945575-17-3
    1. Koger, Fred, 1924–   . 2. World War, 1939–
1945—Aerial operations, American. 3. World War,
1939–1945—Personal narratives, American. 4. United
States. Army Air Forces. Bombardment Group, 92nd.
5. Bombardiers—United States—Biography. I. Title.
D790.K57   1990
940.54′213—dc20   90-37023
                                              CIP

First Printing

10 9 8 7 6 5 4 3 2 1

To Sara, who first went out with me one month after my last trip to Merseburg, and never stopped. She has been my encouragement, my proofreader, my wife, and the love of my life. This book is as much hers as mine.

CONTENTS

This book is the result of a series of happenstances. In October 1980 my wife and I were invited to see an exhibition of aviation art at a local Dallas gallery. The invitation mentioned that General Adolf Galland, former chief of Luftwaffe Fighter Forces, would be present. So we went, and I took along a couple of things I hoped the general would autograph. One was a book, the other an aircraft painting that I had commissioned several years earlier. It was a rendering of an Me-163 rocket fighter. The general was kind enough to autograph both, and was curious to know my interest in the Messerschmitt. I explained that I had an encounter with the fearsome little fighter over Merseburg in August of 1944, and we had quite a conversation about the plane and its effectiveness.

Another guest at the show, Mark Young, took a photograph of my wife and me with the general. Mark was at the time a sergeant in the U.S. Air Force. He offered to send me a print of the photo, and during our conversation asked which group I flew with. I said, "The Ninety-second," and he immediately asked, "Did you know Charlie Hodges?" My reaction was a startled, "How the hell did you know about Charlie Hodges?" I hadn't heard Charlie's name in years, but it was one of the very first names I heard during my first days with the Ninety-second. Even then the story of his exploit over Hamburg was already becoming a Group legend.

Mark said that he lived in Xenia, Ohio, and had bought his home through Charlie's real estate firm. Charlie's exploit was well known to Mark who, being in the Air Force, was somewhat of an aviation buff. I gave Mark a business card, with a note on the back to Charlie. It just said, "Best wishes from an old 92nd flyer."

A couple of weeks later I got a telephone call from Charlie. I didn't know him personally, and he didn't know me. In fact, his action that had earned him the Distinguished Service Cross happened the day before I flew my first mission. In any case, I had subsequent conversations with

Charlie via telephone and letter, and I pushed him to write an account of his experiences with the Eighth Air Force. He seemed interested in the possibility, but it was one of those things he just didn't get around to doing.

Three years later I had about given up on getting Charlie to write his book. But my interest in the Eighth, and in the Ninety-second Bomb Group, had become aroused to the point that one evening I told Sara, "Doggone it, if Charlie won't write *his* book, I think I'll write my own."

Sara said, "Great, why don't you?"

"Well, I didn't do anything at all like Charlie did," I said. "He got the D.S.C. and he should have had a Congressional Medal!"

Sara pointed out that I could still write a book. I did fly thirty-five missions, and I did get shot at many times, and I did come back in some B-17s that shouldn't have made it back. So why not?

I got out my old mission log, rummaged through photographs I had collected over the years, and finally arrived at what I wanted to do—try to describe what it had been like to fly with the Mighty Eighth. Not from the perspective of those high-level people who were involved with the Doctrine of Daylight Bombing, or the selection of priority targets, but a view of the air war as experienced by a very unsophisticated twenty-year-old who had wanted to do it and survive. That's what this book is about, that and nothing more—the story of a small part of the air war in Europe, as I saw it and did it.

Sadly, the man whose heroic action inspired me to start on the book died before its publication. Charlie Hodges suffered a heart attack in October 1987 on his way to a class reunion at Texas A & M University. The massive coronary did what the German flak guns and fighters couldn't do.

Thousands upon thousands of men did just what I did. They climbed into a B-17 or a B-24 and flew it to places where it was definitely not welcome. I hope I have succeeded in picturing a little of what it was like to do that. Although I may not have been aware of it at the time, there was nothing I would rather have done during World War II than be a part of the Mighty Eighth.

Fred Koger

PODINGTON

I leaned against a corner of the old control tower and watched as Sara carefully picked her way across the clods of the plowed field. She stopped a couple of times to aim the Pentax toward me and look through the viewfinder. Finally she found a spot where the composition suited her. She aimed the camera and issued the customary instructions, "Come on now, honey, *smile!*"

But I didn't want to smile. I wanted to look serious. Actually, I wanted to look like a dashing, devil-may-care flier posing briefly for a photo before climbing into a B-17 and roaring off to some distant and dangerous German target. I thrust my left hand into my pocket and crossed my legs.

Sara pressed the shutter release and moved to another spot to get a different view. I thought about warning her that she was standing right in the middle of the perimeter track and had better watch out for taxiing B-17s. I gazed across the plowed field toward the main runway and tried to visualize what it looked like forty years ago. It was a silly thing for a sixty-year-old man to be doing, coming thousands of miles to wallow in nostalgia and try to recapture the feeling of those exciting days forty years ago. But I was enjoying every minute.

I walked out into the field and took the camera. "Now you stand by the tower and let me take your picture," I said. Sara smiled and picked her way back across the stubble. The control tower looked more familiar to me from this vantage point. I had seen it from here so many times, peering through the Plexiglas nose of a B-17 as we taxied along this strip . . . or rather, what *used to be* this strip.

Of all the buildings that once cluttered this old air base, this is the one I had hoped was still standing. It was glamorous and made the base look just like the war movies pictured air bases during the war. And it still looked pretty good, all things considered. Abandoned and neglected, it had survived forty English winters since I'd last seen it. It looked lonely, desperately lonely, standing in that barren field in the

English Midlands. But that's fitting, I thought. The control tower is all that remains, a sort of monument to the Ninety-second Bomb Group. And a monument should look somber, even sad.

I walked across the field toward the main runway, now used on summer Sundays for drag racing automobiles. The secondary runways were gone, along with the perimeter strip and the fifty-two hardstands dispersed along its meandering path. As I walked I tried to remember the way it once looked . . . thousands of yards of concrete stretching and circling, surrounded by hardstands connected to the perimeter by short taxi strips. And, sitting on each hardstand, a huge silver bomber, with a bold white "B" in a black triangle adorning the fin. The marking made the planes look even more deadly and defiant.

I decided not to walk all the way to the runway. Just across it I could see the number two hangar. But number one was closer, just up the road from the tower. No sense walking a mile just to see a strip of concrete and an old hangar. And the runway had probably been resurfaced by now, anyway. I walked back and joined Sara. She was poking around the tower with Leighton Price, whose taxi had transported us along the roads that I once traveled on my bicycle. Leighton asked what else I'd like to see.

"I'd like to see the briefing room, but it's long gone," I said. "But hell, it was just an over-sized Quonset hut, like the other buildings. And they're gone too."

We spent another hour strolling around the area, looking for other tangible evidence that this was once a Combat Bomb Group. I was filled with a pleasant sadness. Shortly before making this trip back in time, I had read a book describing these old air bases. The foreword made reference to "the fascination of these sad places—long after the battle." Whoever wrote that felt exactly the way I felt that day.

As we walked up the road, with me occasionally venturing off through the weeds to look at old sheet iron that marked the barracks site where we lived, Leighton asked, "Were you on the Schweinfurt raid?" I knew exactly which one he meant. He was referring to that "black Tuesday," August 17, 1943. That was the day 188 B-17s battled their way to bomb the German ball bearing plants along the Regnitz River and fought one of the bloodiest battles in the history of air warfare. When it was over thirty-six B-17s were shot down, three crash-landed, and 118 were damaged. Three-hundred-sixty-seven men were killed, wounded, or missing.

"No, Leighton, that was before my time."

I didn't elaborate. Everyone asks about Schweinfurt when they learn I flew with the Eighth Air Force. But I flew in 1944, when the Eighth was at the peak of its power, the peak of it destructiveness. We didn't have to fight our way to the target and back, without escort fighters to help us beat off the savage attacks by Messerschmitts, although we *did* have to fly slowly and unerringly through flak barrages of more than a thousand guns. And we could, and did, drop more than 3,000 tons of bombs on German targets in a single day. The gallant crews who suffered so much at Schweinfurt put just over 400 tons on the targets.

My missions were flown with the "Mighty Eighth." It wasn't so "mighty" when those 188 planes went to Schweinfurt; those were the pioneers who opened the way for the greatest air strike force in history. When I flew with the Eighth we could put more than a thousand heavy bombers over Germany in a single day. And we could do it day after day. Our destructive power was awesome, incredible. It was the air force envisioned by "Hap" Arnold, Jimmy Doolittle, and the other adamant advocates of daylight precision bombing.

There is no doubt that missions were less hazardous in 1944, with our huge force of bombers escorted to the target and back by long-range fighters. B-17s still blew up in giant fireballs or slid slowly away with wings blown off. They still limped home with engines "feathered" and controls shot away, with dead or wounded crewmen aboard. There were just so many of us that the percentages had to be lower.

There have been times when I wondered what it would have been like to fly those early-day missions, when daylight bombing was such a tentative, almost suicidal, undertaking. But if I *had* flown on those early missions, maybe I wouldn't be writing this book.

As Leighton's taxi started back up the road to the village, I looked back at the old control tower, a "last look," as it were. Then across from the tower I saw a large sign, posted as a warning to spectators at the Sunday drag races. It said, "CAUTION—MOTOR RACING CAN BE DANGEROUS!" I mused that, with a slight change in the wording, that sign would have been appropriate forty years ago.

ONE

MILK RUN

I jumped off the back of the truck onto the concrete hardstand, clumsy in my heavy sheepskin flying boots, grabbed the rest of my gear—parachute bag, Mae West life jacket, leather helmet, and oxygen mask—and walked toward the big silver B-17. It looked unusually clean and shiny in the morning sunlight. Today was going to be a pretty day. It should be, I thought, it's almost mid-August. But in England, summer days were not so recognizable as they were back in Texas.

The nose hatch door was open and I started heaving my gear into the plane. I tossed everything as far forward as I could so I could squirm through without having to kick things out of the way. Getting into the nose compartment of a B-17 is tricky, like doing chin-ups on a bar while sliding through an obstacle-course pipe. I grabbed the top of the hatch with both hands, tested my weight on it a couple of times, then swung my legs up through the hatch. Hanging by my hands and heels five feet above the concrete, I wriggled into the opening, sat up, and began pushing my gear up forward.

Crouching behind the seat, I carefully stowed everything just so— the Mae West laid out on top of the fifty-caliber ammo locker on the right side, parachute pack on top of the Mae West with the harness rings up and the rip cord handle to the right. It was as if I had done this a thousand times before. I climbed into the seat and began to check the bombardier's panel and the chin turret control column. Automatically, without consciously thinking about it, I went through the familiar motions and it struck me that I felt very comfortable in this little compartment, very much at home. I leaned forward and scanned the big Plexiglas nose cone to be sure it was clean.

This would be my eighteenth combat mission. I was one mission short of being halfway through my tour. When I got back this afternoon, I would be more than halfway through. It would be downhill from here, after I finished this one.

I sat in the nose for a while, reflecting on how I happened to be sitting here, getting ready to go drop bombs on France, on a Sunday morning, August 13, 1944, almost exactly two months since I arrived at the Ninety-second.

I had begun my adventure with the Eighth Air Force's Ninety-second Bombardment Group back in June. I began as a gunner, trained in armament, and was part of a ten-man bomber crew when I arrived at the Group. Ten days ago, on August 3, that crew had been shot down over Germany. I wasn't with them due to a quirk of fate that occurred shortly after our arrival at the Ninety-second: I had joined another crew as a bombardier.

In an effort to build the Eighth Air Force rapidly into the huge strike force that it had become, many changes were being made. One was the reduction of crew size from ten to nine men. It was decided, correctly, that having two waist gunners was not necessary. Fighter attacks had decreased with the advent of our long-range escort fighters, which could take us all the way to the target and stay with us some of the way home. In the tight confines of the midsection of a B-17, the two waist gunners got in each other's way. So eliminating one waist gunner provided personnel for the formation of additional crews. Copilots with a little experience were made first pilots and given their own crews, replaced by new, inexperienced co-pilots. Gunners were transferred to new crews, and incoming personnel were assigned as individuals rather than entire crews.

The creation of new combat crews required, among other things, more bombardiers—or "toggleers," as we referred to ourselves, since everyone followed the lead plane and dropped when he dropped. So I applied for a job as a bombardier, and got it. I continued to share the hut with the guys from my original crew, and some from other crews because it wasn't considered necessary for a crew to live together. Assignments for a mission might, and often did, result in nine guys who didn't even know one another flying together on a given day. A man with a bad cold had to be replaced; a mission might be alerted with two or three crew members in London on a pass. Things were different from the early days of the Eighth, when ten men flew the entire tour together, although even then there had been replacements for men killed or wounded.

I wondered if some of the glamour had gone out of combat flying. Or was there ever any glamour there to begin with? There was certainly no glamour for my original crew ten days ago when they were chewed to pieces by German flak and fighters.

So I was sitting here, alive, ready to go drop more bombs on the enemy, and my old crew was down somewhere in Germany, either dead or in prison camp. And it was all just luck, pure luck.

I heard a thud on the floor behind me, and turned around to see the navigator's parachute bag. Then came his brown leather briefcase, followed by the thump of his flying boots on the floor. He grunted a couple of times as he wiggled his lanky frame through the hatch, then sat cross-legged on the floor at the back of the compartment. He looked exhausted from the effort.

I said, "Morning, Jack."

"Yeah, good morning. How's it going?"

"Don't know—just got here myself. Looks like a milk run, though."

"Well, you never can tell."

Jack, better known as "Cactus Jack," was one of the most easygoing people I'd flown with. He was from Colorado, and his laconic personality reminded me of Gary Cooper. He was quiet and I had never seen him excited. It was my private opinion that he could curl up under his little navigation table and *sleep* through the bomb run. Nothing seemed to ruffle him. Jack and I had flown several missions together, and I couldn't have picked a more agreeable companion to share the little compartment in the nose.

He got into his seat, facing his table on the left side, and opened his briefcase. He pulled out a couple of navigation charts and put them on the table. I leaned back and looked into the briefcase.

"Lots of sharp pencils, I see, like all good navigators carry."

"Go to hell. Just take care of your switches!"

This exchange was routine, my kidding him about his sharp pencils and his pretending to be pissed off about it. Actually, Jack was a "Mickey" (radar) navigator, and a good one. He used the "G-box" above his table with great expertise, making sense out of the little white blips on the green tube. He had shown me how it worked a couple of times, but I couldn't make heads or tails of it.

"Let's go downstairs and see what's going on," I suggested.

We dropped through the hatch and walked over to where the copilot was handing out the escape kits. These little plastic cases, shaped to fit into the knee pocket of our flight coveralls, contained silk maps, currency, morphine Syrettes, Benzedrine, and other necessities for shot-down fliers. I took mine and said I'd like to get into it and take some of the goodies for souvenirs. He said, "I gotta sign for these damn things, so don't fool with it!"

We paired off and pulled the big props through a couple of turns to clear the lower cylinders, then had an informal get-together and waited for the green flare from the tower. We were all in a jovial mood, mainly because of today's target assignment. We were going to France to provide "battle area support" for the Allied ground offensive. That creates a far different mood than a mission to some oil refinery deep in Germany, with a thousand or more flak guns defending it. Today's mission we classified as a "milk run."

Our ground forces were producing spectacular results this month. After a lengthy slug-fest on the Cherbourg peninsula, the Allied armies had broken out of Normandy and were fighting their way through Brittany. Their momentum was increasing; every day on the BBC War News there was speculation on the liberation of Paris. A couple of days ago I heard a BBC commentator say, "All of France may well be liberated before the month is out, and our armies shall stand on the borders of Germany itself."

I had been keeping up with the battle at Falaise Gap. Our armies had bushwhacked the Germans in the Gap and were trying to encircle them and finish them off. I made a mental note to get one of Jack's maps and find out where the hell Falaise Gap was.

"Start number one."

"Mesh number one."

Each engine of the B-17 started with a whine, a cough, a grinding protest that climbed the scale gradually to a roar. Shorty ran the engines up to full power; I could feel the B-17 straining against the locked brakes. Shorty's voice crackled over the Intercom, "Ready to taxi— check in, crew." The "rogers" started with the tail gunner and ended with me.

Our B-17 started to move, slowly, sluggishly. Shorty held the left brake and revved three and four, turning a little left, aiming for the short taxiway that led to the perimeter strip. A taxiing B-17 moved past us on the perimeter and we waited for it to clear. I tossed a half-salute, half-wave as it passed, then we taxied out and fell in behind it.

A B-17 on the ground is a lumbering, ponderous, over-loaded machine, showing none of the grace and beauty it has in flight. Gazing at the line of bombers moving slowly and awkwardly down the perimeter, stopping and starting in little jerks, I thought they looked like a line of ungainly circus elephants. All that would change in just a few minutes.

"OK, we're up next—get ready for takeoff."

My stomach tightened and I felt the tension build up in my body, as always. The engines ran up to full power, the thunder surrounded me, and everything I looked at blurred with vibration. Then I could feel the quick jolt as the brakes unlocked and we started to move down the runway. The vibration stopped, now just the smooth roar of power as we used up more and more of the runway. Damn, why did I sweat takeoffs so much?

We finally lifted off the runway, and I leaned forward in the nose and looked back to see the left main gear easing up into the engine nacelle. At this point I always had the feeling that we were neither flying nor *not* flying; the plane was deciding whether to keep climbing or just ease back down to the ground. This was not just a phobia of mine. A B-17 is tons of metal, gasoline, bombs, guns, and people—a lot of weight to get into the air. And I was convinced that there was just barely enough power, and barely enough runway, to get airborne. I was sure that most crewmen felt that way, and I was certain the bombardiers did, sitting in the nose and watching the end of the runway come closer and closer.

Then we were climbing into the summer sky and the tenseness went away. I leaned forward and watched the panorama of B-17s, hundreds of B-17s, circling and forming up into groups over the green English Midlands. I looked at the altimeter on my panel—7,000 feet. The ground below was a patchwork of a dozen shades of green. Ahead was the Channel, sometimes gray, and cold, and treacherous, but today deep blue and calm. A few minutes after we crossed the English coast, I pressed the Intercom button: "Bombardier to pilot, OK if I arm the bombs?"

"Roger, bombardier, go ahead."

Swinging my seat around, I made my way back toward the tunnel under the flight deck, trying not to step on Jack's feet. The engineer was standing behind the pilot's seat and he moved over so I could squeeze through. I made my way around the turret and into the bomb bay. I proceeded very carefully now, because the only place to stand was the narrow catwalk that is the "keel" of a B-17, a steel girder about eight inches wide. Walking it in my big flight boots was tricky. I was very deliberate in my movements, like a tightrope walker. I was working without a net. It was impossible to wear a parachute pack and get through the bomb racks, and the bomb bay doors would support only about fifty or sixty pounds before they popped open. Falling was 100 percent fatal.

The operation itself was quite routine. Grab the bomb rack with one hand, lean down and start pulling the cardboard tags from the nose fuses. Each tag is attached to a cotter pin that secures the protective cover over the fuse. With the pin removed, the small propeller on the front of the cover spins off in the air when the bomb is released, exposing the detonating fuse.

I finished the nose fuses and stuffed the pins into the right knee-pocket of my flight suit, then squeezed between the bomb racks and repeated the procedure on the tail fuses. It was a little more difficult to get to them, reaching inside the fins of the bombs. Finished, I took a look at the shackles, and opened the radio room door. I yelled at the radio operator, "What the hell you doing back here, hiding?" He flipped me the finger and I closed the door and carefully made my way back forward.

Back in my seat in the nose, I felt like I had just come up from the depths of a tunnel into the daylight. What a view! I wondered how the radioman stood it, back in that dark little room, not seeing what was going on around us in the sky. Maybe he liked it that way, who knows? Maybe he didn't want to see what was taking place outside. But being confined like that would have driven me nuts.

I settled back in my seat and watched the other B-17s in the formation. The lead plane was about thirty yards in front of us, and a little above our altitude. We stayed a few yards below his flight path so we didn't fly in his prop wash. I could see the tail gunner's face clearly. The barrels of his two fifty-caliber machine guns were pointed slightly upward, and I could see him move them from left to right occasionally.

Just to the right, a bit ahead and above our plane was the deputy lead. If the lead plane was hit and had to drop out of the formation, the deputy lead would swing into position and we would continue the bomb run without missing a step.

The idea of each B-17 carrying a Norden bombsight had long ago been abandoned in favor of selecting a bombardier to serve as lead for a squadron. The other eleven bombardiers in a squadron watched his bomb bay and hit the toggle switch when his bombs went. Hence the term "toggleer." The deputy lead carried a bombsight and the bombardier operated the sight during the bomb run, just as if he were the lead. If nothing happened to the lead plane, he toggled like the rest of us. If the lead went out of action, he just continued the bomb run and we dropped as if nothing had happened.

I watched the number two plane, and it seemed close enough that I might reach out and touch it. It was a magnificent airplane, a great silver bird rising and falling a little as it flew, like a speedboat plowing through choppy water—majestic, deadly, bristling with machine guns and filled with bombs, designed for destruction. But it was so beautiful!

As I watched the deputy lead, my mind drifted back to the morning's briefing. Tom Crosby, a good friend since our training days in gunnery school, was in the nose of that plane. He was one of the last to come into briefing this morning and rather than walk down the center aisle to one of the empty seats up front, he just squatted down beside my seat on the left-hand side of the room. We chatted idly and lit our cigarettes, waiting for the brass to come in and get the show on the road.

When the G-2 officer pulled the curtains open on the big map, I nudged Tom and grinned.

"France again," Tom said, a smile lighting up his square face. "You fly yesterday?"

"Yeah, Paris. Wonder how long these milk runs will last."

"A while, I hope."

I agreed and said, "It's nice to get in a few of these. Last month was all Germany for me."

The briefing had begun and we stopped talking.

"Today the Eighth Air Force will provide battle-area support for the Allied ground forces. Your Primary Target is the German supply depot here"—he jabbed the map with his pointer—"just outside Evreux, France."

The mood in the briefing room was relaxed and cheerful. The whispered comments were made with a smile. It was not at all like the uneasy mumbling when the target was way to hell inside Germany and G-2 was warning us about "moderate to intense flak." There was joy in briefing rooms all over England this morning.

"Pilot to crew, 10,000 feet, time to go on oxygen."

My mask was already snapped onto the left side of my leather flying helmet. I pulled it over my face and hooked it onto the other side. The rubber mask felt ice-cold against my face. In a little while it would be warm and wet from my breath.

We were well into France when I called for an oxygen check. The crew's voices crackled over the intercom . . . "Tail gunner OK." "Waist OK." "Ball turret OK." "Radio OK." "Top turret OK." "Flight deck OK." "Navigator, Roger."

It was a beautiful summer day over France. Only patches of white cummulus clouds and the contrails made by squadrons of B-17s marked the blue August sky. France rolled by beneath us in a crazy quilt pattern of greens and browns, a town here and there, an occasional river to break up the pattern. I stared at the ground and wondered what the fighting was like down there. Air combat, if you're lucky, is just a terrifying fifteen or twenty minutes over the target, then the trip home. On the ground, I thought, it was constant maneuvering for position, or waiting for a bomb strike or an artillery barrage, or hugging the inside of a foxhole until the enemy artillery stopped. From 20,000 feet it was hard for me to realize that battles were being fought down there.

"Pilot to crew, I.P. coming up in fifteen minutes. Get the flak suits on."

I wondered if I really needed to put the damn thing on today. There probably wouldn't be any flak. But I saw Jack wrestling with his heavy body armor and swiveled my seat around to help him. He handed me the front and back pieces of my suit and helped me snap the Dzus fittings on the shoulders. Turning my seat forward again, I figured I weighed about 300 pounds. Oh hell, I can take it off again in a few minutes.

"Pilot to crew, I.P. in two minutes."

"Bombardier to crew, oxygen check." More "OKs" and "Rogers" from tail to front.

I could see the I.P. (Initial Point) just ahead, a town east of Evreux.

Visibility was good, just a little haze between us and the ground, and a few scattered clouds here and there. I pulled my goggles down over the oxygen mask for better vision.

"Turning on the I.P." We made an easy swing to the left, still holding a nice, tight formation. We levelled off and I pulled off my heavy flying gloves, leaving them hanging by the electric cords attached to the sleeves of the heated suit. My eyes were glued to the lead plane. His bomb bay doors started to come open and I pushed my own door lever.

"Bomb bay doors coming open!"

"Bomb doors fully open." This from the radio operator, who could open his door and look directly into the bomb bay.

"Thanks, radio!"

I turned my seat a little to the left and flipped the switches on the bombardier's panel. Rack selectors on. Intervalometer on. Set for two-hundred feet. Toggle switch safety removed.

I looked back up at the lead plane, then glanced over to number two. Tom would have his sight warmed up by now and I pictured him hunched over it, his right eye tight against the soft black rubber eye-piece.

I looked quickly back to the lead plane. No bombs yet. I never took my eyes off the lead plane for more than a couple of seconds. I always worried about dropping late. A bombardier could sit there half hypno-tized and not react instantly when the lead dropped. This is known as "head up ass and locked." I had never dropped late and didn't intend to start now.

Five minutes into the bomb run—still a while to go. A glance at the panel to be sure everything was on. My left hand wrapped around the junction-box, ready to slap the toggle switch on top.

I heard a "pop" that sounded like a faraway pistol shot and felt a sudden warmth on my face. What the hell was going on? My eyes snapped to the right, and there was Crosby's B-17 . . . upside down! Jesus, the right wing was *gone*! Completely gone! I continued to stare, and couldn't believe what I was seeing. A B-17 upside down! Then I saw the harsh red flames streaking back from where the wing used to be, blurring the shape of the fuselage.

For an eternity the doomed B-17 seemed to hang there as if it wanted to stay with the formation. Then it started to slide away, and in an instant it was gone.

I looked back up at the lead plane. I felt completely numb. Not scared, just numb. I sensed Jack standing behind me and glanced over my right shoulder. He was crouched at the window on the right and he looked up when I turned my head. His eyes were as big as saucers. Good old unflappable Jack was shook. His eyes had a stunned, unbelieving look. A look of horror.

I looked back at the lead and watched his bomb bay doors until finally a couple of bombs floated lazily downward. I hit the toggle switch, mechanically, still thinking about Crosby's plane being upside down. Our plane bucked upwards and I guess I yelled, "Bombs away!"

Then we were banking away from the target and I called for an oxygen check.

It must have been five minutes before anyone said anything about what had happened. Then somebody's voice on the intercom said, "Christ, did you see what happened to number two?"

"Yeah, he took a direct hit!"

"I saw the right wing stand straight up and come off!"

"I didn't even see any flak."

"I did. Three or four bursts, just below us."

"That was Brechbill's crew, wasn't it?"

"Yeah. They were about ready to start flying lead."

Laurence Brechbill was a West Point graduate. He may have been the only man in the Group to wear proper military uniform at all times. I'm *sure* he was the only one who still had the grommet in his cap. He didn't think the "fifty-mission crush" was appropriate! I had only seen him a few times, didn't know him at all. But I knew Crosby, and he was the first close friend I had actually seen go like that.

The trip back was short and the intercom was mostly silent. It was still a beautiful day over France, but all I could visualize was that burning B-17 hanging upside down right beside us. I kept thinking about Tom, hunkered down over his bombsight. I wondered if he ever knew what hit him. Maybe he was alive and rode the burning plane all the way down.

Our tires squealed on the runway, and I was leaning forward in the nose, looking back to see the left wheel start rolling. I always did this, and today was no different.

When I entered the mission in my log, I added a brief comment, "Rough—Crosby had it today." I looked over the seventeen missions before today. Some of them had flak so thick you could walk on it. Today the flak was hardly worth noticing. Just one or two batteries, probably. Doing what they were supposed to do, just as we were.

August 13 started out as "the day of the milk runs." Seven-hundred-fifty-seven B-17s bombed dozens of "Evreuxs" all over France . . . Saint-Malo, Le Manoir Bridge, Ile de Cezembre. None of the dreaded names like Hamburg, Munich, Berlin. But over these "milk run" targets 7 B-17s were shot down, 1 crash-landed in England, and 484 came home with battle damage.

The official report issued by the Ninety-second said, "The aircraft piloted by Second Lieutenant Laurence M. Brechbill failed to return, and the crew is missing in action."

TWO

E.T.O.

I t was the morning of May 13, 1944, that I first felt that I was really in the war. Standing at the port rail of a troop ship, one day out of Boston harbor, I gazed out across the gray-green waters of the North Atlantic, catching an occasional glimpse of other ships in the convoy as they appeared and disappeared in the ocean swells. It was a scene right out of a Humphrey Bogart movie I'd seen just a few months ago.

Our convoy must have covered fifty square miles of ocean. There were tankers, freighters, troop ships, and Navy destroyers. The nearest ship to ours was straight off our port side, a troop ship like ours, as well as I could make it out. None of us had been told how many ships were in the convoy. The trip would take about two weeks.

Everything up to now had been a training exercise, every battle situation had been simulated. But that was past. From now on everything was real. Those destroyers were not on a training cruise, they were there to protect this convoy. The Navy gun crew on the ship looked as if they took their job seriously as they sprinted to battle stations, always timed by a petty officer with a stopwatch. And if they actually had to fire their deck cannons, it wouldn't be at a tow-target.

I was excited, and enjoying this immensely. Hell, this is what I'd been wanting to do ever since we got into the war. At least it's what I *thought* I wanted to do.

Even before Pearl Harbor, when it was obvious that we were going to get involved in the war, I wanted to get into the Army Air Corps. I had been reading airplane magazines like *Air Trails* since I was twelve, and had built model airplanes representing most of the World War I types. What little I knew about aviation, from magazines and movies, was about military aviation. I wasn't terribly interested in the commercial airliners or the China Clippers. I was fascinated by people like Jimmy Doolittle flying the fast and dangerous little Gee-Bees in the Thompson Trophy races. But military airplanes were the big thing, and my interest had shifted during the last two or three years from fighters to bombers.

A close friend of mine from my home town of Waxahachie, Texas had given me some firsthand knowledge about the Air Corps, and bombers, and combat. J. B. Colleps was about two years older than me, and enlisted in the Air Corps about the time we got into the war. In mid-1942 he was home on leave, wearing bombardier wings and an air medal. He had just finished a combat tour in the Aleutians, flying B-25s. I spent all the time I could with J. B., listening to his stories of early morning takeoffs in the cold Aleutian fog, and popping open the bomb bay doors to drop his deadly cargo through a break in the clouds. I was absolutely spellbound, and he convinced me beyond a doubt that flying in bombers was the only way to fight the war.

I enlisted right after I turned eighteen, but then wasn't called to active duty until six months later. Not long after I left for the Air Corps my mother sent me a letter and a newspaper clipping about J. B. He had been killed while flying as an instructor on a night training mission at Midland, Texas. This hit me as the ultimate irony; to survive the hazards of combat, and the terrible Aleutian weather he had to fly in, only to die on the Texas prairie in an AT-11.

J. B. was the second close friend I'd lost in the war. George Yarbrough, a guy that I had known since childhood, had enlisted in the Navy when he was barely seventeen. He had been home on leave once, and tried to talk me into going into the Navy, but I was holding out until I was eighteen. I just had to get in the Air Corps. George was aboard the USS *Marblehead* and was killed in one of the Pacific naval battles. The war didn't seem quite so glamorous when I got news like that.

I don't think any of my close friends were drafted into service, they all enlisted voluntarily, as I did. But every city and town in America had a draft board to make sure that able-bodied men between eighteen and thirty answered the call to duty. Hundreds of thousands of men across America received telegrams that began "Greetings from the President of the United States . . . "

After that "day that would live in infamy," December 7, 1941, the United States changed literally overnight from an isolationist country that wanted no part of another European war. There was a national singleness of purpose: to put an end forever to the totalitarian nations that threatened to rule the world. Patriotism in America didn't just flourish, it raged. Factories were converted almost overnight to producing materials for war. Scrap drives produced every conceivable kind of material—scrap rubber for tires, aluminum pots and pans to build airplanes, scrap iron for guns and bombs. The old street car tracks in Waxahachie were ripped up and sent off to war.

The American people had an unquestioning willingness to devote their energies to winning the war. The young men enlisted and some of the young women too. People who didn't have to work went to work in war plants. My father, who had never worked for another person in his life, was working as a riveter at North American Aviation. He was building B-24 bombers, which I fervently hoped I would never have to fly—not because my dad worked on them, but they just weren't nearly the combat airplane the B-17 was.

America was at war, totally and unconditionally. But the war wasn't taking place in America. The battles were being fought in faraway "Theaters of Operation" like China, Burma, India, Africa, Europe. I was now on the way to one of those theaters, the European Theater of Operations, always referred to by the military as the E.T.O.

Back home, a theater was still a place you went to see a movie. Nowadays, it was often a war movie. That's where I had gotten my impressions of what the war was like. *Life* magazine provided some of the graphic images of the war that were still imprinted on my brain. I kept one issue, reading and re-reading it until it was almost worn out. It had a front-cover photograph of an English Spitfire pilot. Inside were dozens of pictures of determined young pilots in leather jackets and white silk scarves sprinting toward their planes and roaring down grass-strip runways to do battle with the Luftwaffe, even though they were always out-numbered, twenty to one or forty to one. I memorized their names—Cobber Cain, Bob Stanford-Tuck, "Leo the Lion" Clisby, Mahaddie, Beamont. Damn, what a glamorous way to fight a war!

So far, though, my entry into the war, or at least toward the war zone, hadn't been so glamorous. I was not roaring off into the wild blue yonder, but standing at the rail of a troop ship, plowing through the North Atlantic at a speed of about ten knots.

The routine of shipboard life was about as slow-paced as the convoy itself. I spent the days in a lackadaisical ritual that didn't vary much from one day to the next, playing poker or blackjack for small stakes and, tiring of that, just standing on deck for long periods gazing out at the sea and reflecting on whatever came to mind. The salt-water showers always made me feel dirtier after the shower than before. The daily lifeboat drill broke the monotony a bit, but not much. I talked sometimes with the Navy gun crew guys, who bitched constantly about how much the Merchant seamen were being paid and how little the Navy guys got.

The Cokes we bought in the ship's store were never chilled. I scrounged a long piece of heavy cord from one of the seamen and tried my own method of chilling them. I'd tie the string tightly around the neck of the bottle and lower it down the side of the ship, hoping to drag it through the cold North Atlantic water. It couldn't be done, but I kept trying, just to have something to occupy my time. The Coke bottle would hit the water and bounce up the side of the ship. I'd lower it again and it would bounce up the side again. This continued until either the bottle broke against the ship or else I gave up, hauled it in, and drank the contents at air temperature.

During the two-week voyage we received absolutely no news of what was going on in the war or in the world for that matter. There had been rumors of a coming invasion of France, but I didn't put much stock in them. My impression was that the entire French, Belgian, and Dutch coastline was wall-to-wall German artillery and Panzer divisions. We did have troops on the ground in Europe, however. Italy had been invaded months before, and our troops were stubbornly fighting their way toward Rome. But the last news I heard before we boarded the troop ship was that we were stalled at the Rapido River. Whatever was going on in Europe, we would just have to wait until we got to England to find out.

Most of the "passengers" on our ship were Army Air Corps, some of them combat crew personnel, some ground crew. We "fly boys" stayed pretty much together. I had nothing against the "paddlefeet," as we termed most everybody who didn't fly, but I got the feeling from time to time that the ground guys thought we felt superior to them. They seemed to feel that we had too much rank, got too many medals, and acted a bit too cocky. Maybe we did, I don't know.

Our particular little "group" was made up of twenty men, two combat crews who had trained together briefly at Dalhart, Texas. We had come by train to Boston and we lived together aboard the ship. I got to know my own crew a little better during the trip. We had more time to spend talking and learning how we felt about things. We discussed everything from girls to combat flying to our home towns. We hadn't been together as a crew but for a few weeks, and during final phase training didn't have time for much but learning what we were supposed to do on a B-17. Our phase training in Dalhart was cut short, which didn't displease us in the least. We had flown perhaps a half dozen practice missions when we were asked if we'd like to "accelerate" our departure for the E.T.O. We responded to this with a ten-man "Hell, yes!"

Based on the movies I'd seen, a combat crew was supposed to be a close-knit, one-for-all and all-for-one team. I didn't think we fit that description, but then we scarcely knew each other yet. We got along fine, but I'm not sure how many of us would have become friends if we hadn't been put together as a crew.

Lester, the engineer/top turret gunner, was a big, broad-faced farm boy from the Midwest. He had a friendly openness and an almost naive sincerity about doing his job. He was a very good engineer, but he always seemed eager to learn more and to be sure that what he was doing was right. I thought he underrated his abilities. Most of the time he wore a broad grin.

Moore, the tail gunner, can only be described as irrepressible. He was short, square-faced, with a mop of curly hair, and came from New England. Moore was constantly in motion, talking, gesturing, and singing. He worshipped Bing Crosby, and did a very good job imitating him. He knew every song Crosby ever sang, had seen all his movies, and was currently having a fit to see "Going My Way," which had just been released. I don't think I ever saw Moore stretch out and just relax, or read a book. He was a live wire with an insatiable zest for life. I couldn't imagine anyone not liking him.

Brewer, a gunner, was also from a midwestern farm community. He was quiet and taciturn; he never had much to say, but was pleasant and not at all withdrawn. He was always willing to participate in a conversation, but more as an interested observer than a talker. Like most of us, I don't think he'd been very far from home before he enlisted in the Air Corps.

Horton, another gunner, was a skinny nineteen-year-old with buck teeth and a sullen personality. After a few drinks he tried to be the life of the party, but he just couldn't pull it off. He didn't seem to know much about history, current events, or anything else. And he didn't seem particularly interested in knowing. I don't think his I.Q. was more than the minimum needed to get into the Air Corps, and I must admit that I wouldn't have spent ten minutes with him if he hadn't been a part of the crew.

By far the most interesting of the ten was Hanley, the radio operator. I don't know his exact age but he was at least ten years older than the rest of us—over thirty, I was sure. He was well educated and had done everything from teaching school to working on banana boats to Central America. He didn't inflict stories on us; we had to encourage him. But he wasn't reluctant to talk about his experiences. He had seen and done more than all the rest of us put together. After a while I began to sense, that not all of his experiences while knocking around the country during the Depression years were as much fun as they sounded in the retelling. Even with Hanley's willingness to talk about his life and his experiences, I had the feeling that we really didn't know him.

Hanley always had a lot of money. A lot of money, to me, was anything over a hundred bucks. I'd seen him bet that much in a poker game. I was certain he had income from somewhere besides his Air Corps pay. And I was equally certain that I'd never find out about it— not from him, anyway.

The pilot was a nice looking, well educated fellow from the Pacific northwest. He was sandy-haired, tall, and self-assured. It was easy for me to see why he was chosen as pilot and aircraft commander. The copilot was a lot like Lester, both in his physical appearance and his personality. The rest of the crew I really hadn't gotten to know yet.

We docked at Mersey-side in Liverpool on May 26, 1944, exactly two weeks after leaving Boston harbor. My first look at the English countryside was from the tailgate of a G.I. truck. Our destination was Stone, an Air Corps processing station. It was a pleasant place, not far southwest of Liverpool. We were assigned to very nice quarters, and the paperwork done to process us into the E.T.O. could have been completed in a couple of hours, but we were there for a week. That didn't surprise me; I had learned a long time ago that "hurry up and wait" was more than just an expression. It was the way the military worked, and getting upset about it did absolutely no good.

Leaving the base was no problem at all; we just signed out, and signed back in when we returned. I stayed on the base for two days, then decided to go for a walk in the English countryside. It was already lush and green. I had walked about a mile, dawdling along the country lane, when I met my first English girl. She was riding a bicycle and when I smiled and said "Good morning" she stopped and got off the bike. Her name was Nellie, and she was nice looking. Not a knockout, but cute. We walked along for a while, talking about the usual things—where are you from? when did you get here? what do you do? She had a kind of flirtatious, coquettish way of smiling and lowering her eyes, and I decided she was not exactly opposed to male companionship. But we were in the middle of the countryside, in broad daylight, and I couldn't figure out any way to have a romantic interlude. She finally said she'd better be getting home, and I asked for her address. I promised I'd write when I got to my Bomb Group. She said she'd love to hear from me, and I jotted her name and address in my ever-present, little leather-bound book: Nellie Stokes, No. 7, Chetwynd Street, Smallthorne, Stoke-on-Trent. Walking back to the base, thinking about the way she acted, I was convinced that she had done everything she could to entice me except sing a chorus of "Roll me over in the clover!"

A couple of miles from Stone was a large munitions plant at a place called Eccleshall. According to some of the guys who claimed to have checked it out, there were several thousand women working there and practically no men. And of course the women were all sex-starved and would practically throw you down and attack you. I had serious doubts about this, but the word around Stone was "carry a raincoat with you if you're around Eccleshall at shift-change; grass stains are hard to get out of your uniform." I never carried a raincoat, and never checked to see if it was true about Eccleshall.

On June 2 we got word that we were going to the Combat Crew Center at "The Wash." We took another G.I. truck ride, longer than the trip from Liverpool, and finally stopped at the most bleak and desolate place I had ever seen. "The Wash" turned out to be a large inlet on the North Sea coast, sparsely inhabited and, as far as I was concerned, uninhabitable! Everything was a dull gray color, the land, the sky, the sea, the buildings. And some of the buildings weren't buildings at all, they were tents—big wall-tents; the Army called them squad tents. But what was the Air Corps doing living in tents? That was for the Infantry.

In addition to the comments about how much we hated the place, somebody asked, "What the hell are we supposed to do here?" That was a good question, I thought, and during the next ten days I didn't really get a satisfactory answer. We had so-called "training sessions" daily, mostly lectures. We learned a little about air-war tactics and the objectives of the Eighth Air Force. The only thing interesting or useful, in my opinion, was the informal question-and-answer sessions with some guys who had finished combat tours. I was most interested to hear what they had to say, and so were the others. I got the impression that this "training period" at The Wash was just a way to fill in time until we were needed to replace some crew who had finished their tour or got shot down. There didn't seem to be anything vital or even important about the program.

On June 6 we got news that probably electrified the rest of the world but made us feel even more frustrated. The Allied Forces had invaded Normandy with a huge armada of ships and thousands of men and machines. When we heard the announcement on the base Tannoy speakers we headed for the day room to listen to the details on the radio. The room was a jumble of sound. The BBC announcer was talking about "Omaha Beach . . . Juno . . . Sword . . . thousands of American and British troops pouring ashore . . . no reports yet concerning casualties or enemy resistance. . . . I was concerned that we might have spent the last year and a half training, and then come all the way here, only to miss out on the war. A few guys seemed elated about the Invasion, but most of us were worried about whether we'd ever get into action.

The Air Corps did not forget about us. Five days after the Invasion we got orders to report to U.S.A.A.F. Station 109. We had no idea where in hell that was, but it had to be better than The Wash. On the morning of June 12 we left King's Lynn by train; our destination was Cambridge. It was a month to the day since we left Boston harbor, but to me it seemed like a year. I had been in transit ever since we left Dalhart, Texas, almost two months ago. It was like being in limbo!

We spent the time on the train watching the English countryside from the train windows, and speculating on where we were going, where the Group was located, how far from London; Moore wondered how soon we could get a pass after we got there. I wished that I had brought along a map of England; I had no idea where we were or where we were headed.

About thirty or forty of us got off the train at the station in Cambridge. A transportation officer and a couple of enlisted men met us and briefed us on the situation. We were to be back at the station about four o'clock for transport to our various groups; in the meantime we were told we could spend the day in Cambridge.

We wandered away from the station and gradually divided up into groups of five or six, usually with fellow crew members. I was awed by the picturesque old buildings and the narrow, winding cobblestone streets. Most of the buildings were incredibly ornate, and obviously old, very old. I thought a lot of them were churches, but the plaques indicated they were colleges—colleges that dated from the 1500s and 1600s. The commercial part of the city was intertwined with the colleges, and we window-shopped our way along one street after another. After a time we stumbled onto a small pub with some tables set up on the sidewalk in front and, without anybody saying a word, just automatically walked inside. A nice-looking girl behind the bar smiled and asked what we'd have. Somebody said, "How about a beer?" and the rest of us seconded the motion. The barmaid drew six big mugs of beer, or what appeared to be beer. But it didn't have a foamy head like American draft beer. I asked what kind of beer it was, and she said, "Why it's bitter." I wasn't sure whether she was identifying the beer or describing the taste, but I thanked her and put a shilling on the bar.

We walked outside and sat down at two of the sidewalk tables. The "bitter" wasn't bad at all, just a little watery compared to the beer I was used to.

It was about time that we headed back to the station, so we finished our beers and sauntered back through Cambridge. The trip to U.S.A.A.F. Station 109 was another ride on a G.I. truck. I tried to see as much as I could from the back of the truck, but my impression was a jumble of twisting roads, sharp turns through little villages with the sides of the truck almost scraping the gray stone buildings, and stretches of road so covered with trees that it was like driving through a tunnel.

Finally the truck stopped and we leaned out to see where we were. There was a guard shack sitting by a big sign that said, "FAME'S FAVORED FEW." The M.P. at the gate waved our truck forward. We moved through the gate and bumped along a narrow road, finally stopping in front of a building with a large half-circular sign over the entrance. The sign was ornate and colorful, featuring the Eighth Air Force emblem in the center. At the top it was lettered, "HEADQUAR-TERS—92nd Bomb Group (H)" and at the bottom, "FAME'S FA-VORED FEW." On either side of the entrance was a hundred-pound practice bomb sitting on the fin, with the nose inverted into the top to serve as an ashtray. This added a familiar touch; I'd seen a hundred of these bomb ash trays at training bases in the States.

We got off the truck and put down our B-4 bags as an officer came out to greet us. He gave us a brief welcoming speech, picked up our mimeographed orders, and told us we were assigned to the 326th Squadron. A sergeant escorted us across the road and guided us through a little "village" of Quonset huts that all looked alike. He finally stopped in front of one, checked the number against his assignment sheet, and said, "Here's your new home. Good luck!"

We opened the door and walked inside the little round-roofed corru-gated iron building. Inside the door was a small entry hall with another door leading to the inside. The sergeant followed us inside, explaining that the double doors were to prevent light showing at night. Open one door, close it, then open the other. The blackout was strictly enforced.

The inside of the hut was sparsely furnished, but I thought it was a cozy little place to live. There were six iron beds along each side with plenty of room in between. In the center of the room was an iron potbellied stove, a good-sized table, and half-a-dozen chairs sitting haphazardly around the table. The two bunks at the far left end of the hut were occupied, the rest empty.

We stood for a few minutes, looking around and deciding where we wanted to be. I decided first, and picked the bunk at the far right end. There was a window over it. The window had the usual double cur-tains—blackout curtains. I figured that it would now be my respon-sibility to see that the curtains were closed at night, but I liked being by a window.

I heaved my B-4 bag onto the bunk and sat down beside it. I had lived out of this incredible piece of luggage for more than a month. Now I would unpack it and settle down for a while.

We decided to have a look around the area before we settled in, so we walked outside. Two guys came out of the hut next door and walked over to introduce themselves.

Moore asked, "Where's the mess hall?"

"We're headed over there now—it's the combat mess. Not far."

"How many missions you guys got in?" Moore didn't have any trouble meeting people, and he got right down to asking questions.

"I've got nine. Jerry, you've got eleven, haven't you?"

"Yeah."

"What's it like? Anything exciting happening?"

"You should have been here three weeks ago if you wanted to see some excitement."

"What happened?"

"A damn disaster happened—I thought the bomb dump had blown up. The blast knocked a radio off the shelf in our hut, and the runway's a mile away from here."

The two of them filled us in on this disaster as we walked along to the combat mess. It happened on May 20, and it was the worst disaster in the history of the Group. The weather was terrible that morning; a low-hanging fog shrouded the base, and normally a mission would have been scrubbed. But this was an urgent mission, supposedly, and the B-17s were making an instrument takeoff at fifteen-second intervals. The first plane got off just before seven o'clock. By seven-fifteen, the first squadron was airborne and the second squadron was getting into the air. Half of the twelve B-17s were airborne, but the seventh plane didn't quite make it. It crashed just off the end of the runway. The next plane in line was already halfway down the runway when the pilot was told to abort his takeoff. He jammed on the brakes and brought the plane to a stop just short of the end of the runway.

But the next B-17 in line was roaring down the runway and didn't hear the abort order on his radio. At least that's what everyone assumed. The B-17 that aborted takeoff turned around and started to taxi back down the runway. It taxied into oblivion, colliding with the plane taking off. Each B-17 was carrying six thousand-pound bombs. The bombs started exploding when the two planes collided; there were three separate explosions, then a fourth when the bombs in the first plane to crash off the end of the runway went off.

When it was all over there were twenty men dead. Another died the following day, and nine were in the hospital. And there was a hole in the runway big enough to hold a B-17.

"I'm surprised that anybody got out," I said. "Which Squadron was it?"

"The 326th." Ours.

The conversation in the combat mess was a mixture of jokes, sarcastic "G.I. humor," and occasional comments about that "Black Saturday" three weeks ago. It was still daylight when we left the mess and walked back toward the barracks area. There were six or seven "veterans" with us, and we were strung out along the road in groups, asking questions, trying to find out all we could about life—and death—in the Ninety-second. These veterans were casual about combat flying; they talked about planes shot down in the same offhand way they bitched about powdered eggs.

Back at the hut we got busy arranging our little areas the way we wanted them. I was picky about everything being just so, and when I finished I was very satisfied with my new home. My B-4 bag made a nice "hanging dresser," at the end of the clothing bar, with the big zipper compartments used for underwear, socks, shaving kit and miscellaneous non-G.I. stuff.

The two other fellows who lived in our hut came in about ten o'clock. After the introductions and handshakes we sat around the center of the hut and talked for a while. "How about girls?" Moore, as always, came right to the point.

"Some. Not many. It's just a little burg, and there's more of us than there are of them."

"How do you get there and back?"

"Bicycle. You've gotta have a bicycle to get anywhere, even around the base. Life's too short to wait for a damn truck all the time."

We were up early the next morning. Our indoctrination was a whirlwind affair. By mid-afternoon I had been to a lot of places, told a lot of things, and issued a lot of gear, but I didn't feel like I knew much more than when I arrived. I did know where the squadron office was. And I had the impression that all the information we needed was issued from there. The bulletin board, where the daily postings that affected us were tacked up, was the center of my life from now on. The right side of the board was where the "Mission Alert" was posted, with the names of everybody scheduled to fly the next day. It was up to me, and every other combat crewman, to check it every day. Nobody was going to come find us and tell us whether we were supposed to fly.

I still didn't know my way around the base yet. The layout seemed to be a helter-skelter arrangement of Quonset huts and prefab buildings. And bicycle racks; there were bicycles everywhere. I wondered where the flight line was. I still hadn't seen a B-17.

We heard that the Group was out on a mission and due back any time now. We were through for the day and headed down toward the control tower to watch them come in. We were anxious to see some airplanes— some combat airplanes.

The control tower looked like the ones I'd seen in the war movies. It was a square, two-story building with a black iron railing around the top. The roof was flat, and on the corner nearest the runways was a small cubicle with glass on all four sides. The rest of the roof was cluttered with antennas and assorted meteorology gear. Beyond the tower I could see the runways. There were a lot of people standing around the area. I saw the crash truck and fire engine sitting out near the runways, with the crews sitting on them or stretched out on the grass alongside.

I heard somebody say, "Here they come!" At first they were just specks in the sky, then I could hear a distant drone of engines. As the planes got closer, I couldn't make out a formation; they seemed strung out across the sky. In just seconds the drone became a roar and the first squadron passed over our heads. They were in formation—not a tight combat formation, but still a formation. As they passed overhead, three planes in the low element peeled off, one at a time, at about thirty-second intervals. The first plane swung lazily around and lined up with the runway. As it came closer I could see the big white "B" in the black triangle on the fin, with the red stripe running behind it. The sun glinted on the polished aluminum. It floated in and the tires squealed on the runway. No bounce, just a little wobble from side to side, then it taxied to the end of the runway and turned off. The next plane was almost on the runway when the first one taxied off it. I saw that the two inboard engines of the first plane were now cut off; the props were slowing to a stop. I supposed it was S.O.P. (Standard Operating Procedure) to taxi on just two engines.

I watched every one, occasionally looking up at a squadron turning slowly toward the base, waiting for the first squadron to clear the runway. The fifth plane to land had a prop feathered. I asked the guy standing next to me if that might be engine failure. He said, "Engine failure, my ass—flak, most likely."

I saw two or three B-17s still in the old olive-drab camouflage paint, but most of them were bright silver. Another plane in the first squadron had a feathered prop, but it seemed to be flying just as well on three engines. I'd heard they'd fly on two. As I watched this incredible show, I kept reminding myself that these planes had just been over Europe a few hours ago, being shot at. And some of them hit, apparently.

Somebody said, "There's the 407th."

"Yeah, I see them. Can you make out how many?"

"All of them, I think."

I watched until the last plane was down, and during the process I figured out that there was no "flight line," as there was back in the States. The planes turned off the runway onto a perimeter strip that circled the field and taxied along, finally turning off and parking just off the perimeter. I had heard the word "hardstands," and I assumed these were the parking pads. They were dispersed around the runways, some of them out of sight behind little patches of woods. Trucks were running up and down the perimeter strip, stopping beside the B-17s. I could barely make out the crews piling into the trucks.

After the planes were all down, we stood and talked for a while, as if we were reluctant to leave. The show was over, but we seemed to be waiting for another one to start. Finally we ambled back up the road toward the barracks area.

We learned that the Group had bombed in France that day—tactical targets. One B-17 was shot down, hit by very accurate flak over the target. Somebody said there were nine chutes, so I guess the crew got out OK. There was a lot of battle damage, however, and I wondered how much worse it would be if they had been to Germany instead of France.

As I walked back up the road, thinking about what an awesome sight that was, it suddenly hit me that maybe next time I wouldn't be a spectator. I had a funny, sort of tingling feeling in my stomach. I decided it was excitement. I didn't want to think it was fear.

THREE

INTO BATTLE

The radio in our hut was turned on most of the time. Almost all of the music was American songs played by the big bands— Glenn Miller, Tommy Dorsey, Kay Kyser, Harry James. The song that seemed to be most popular was "I'll Walk Alone," a sentimental lyric sung by a girl whose fella was off to war. She was, of course, being faithful and waiting for him to return. I heard Moore singing the melody with a slightly different lyric. His version went, "I'll Bomb Cologne, With my Mickey and G-box to guide me; With ten-tenths clouds to hide me. . . " I didn't ask him whether he composed the new lyrics or heard them somewhere, but they seemed to me to suit our situation.

We were all interested in the frequent BBC War News reports, which were preceded by a marching song that I quickly learned to like. It was undoubtedly British, had a strong rhythm and a melody that fit my idea of the stoic invincibility of the British. I liked the tune, and after hearing it several times I found myself frequently humming or whistling it. The name of the march was "Into Battle."

I first went into battle on June 19. The lights in our hut came on about four in the morning, and a sergeant with a clipboard started calling out names. We answered to our names in groggy, half-asleep voices. He made sure we were all awake and sitting more or less upright, then called out the time for breakfast, briefing, and oddly, I thought, the fuel-load for today. I don't remember how much fuel we were carrying that first time.

Breakfast in the Combat Mess, briefing, suiting up in the Equipment Room, the truck ride to the hardstand, and pre-flighting the B-17 all went by in sort of a blur. I seemed to be carried along by the activity, just trying to keep up with everything that was going on. In what seemed like just a few minutes, we were in the air and forming up. We headed across the Channel and by the time we reached the French coast the pilot announced on the intercom, "Turning on the I.P." Suddenly our bombs were gone, we were turning away from the coast and back over the

Channel. There was some conversation on the intercom, but not much. I saw the White Cliffs of Dover as we crossed back over the English coast, then we were back on the hardstand. The mission was over almost as fast as it began, and I felt like I hadn't even been anywhere.

We bombed the Pas de Calais, just twenty or so miles across the Channel from Dover. Our target was the V-1 launching sites, from where the Germans were sending the deadly little jet-propelled flying bombs into London. I saw a few puffs of flak, three or four, I think. None of it was really close to our plane. But technically, I had now been shot at —and missed.

We were back in our hut by mid-afternoon. I sat down on the edge of my bunk, reached into my B-4 bag, and got out my little leather address book. I turned the first few pages and decided to begin my mission log on page nine. I checked to be sure there were enough blank pages to record thirty missions. I decided to list the missions on right-hand pages, with the facing left-hand pages used for notations about the missions. I wrote the word "MISSIONS" at the top of the page, with an elaborate curlique design on either side, and then noticed that everything was off-center. Below this I printed three column headings: Number, Date, Place. Then I wondered whether I should have put "Target" instead of "Place." Oh well, a target was a place. I made the first entry: "1—June 19—Pas de Calais."

Ten more blank lines on this first page. The page looked terribly empty. But I had to start somewhere.

We sat around the hut for the next couple of hours, talking sporadically about the day's mission. After dinner we walked back from the combat mess, just dawdling along and making casual conversation. I was wondering if we were going to fly again tomorrow. Some of the veterans I had talked with since we arrived at the Group said that sometimes you'd fly two or three days in a row, then maybe you wouldn't be alerted for the next week or so.

We stopped in the squadron office and tried to look casual as we headed for the right-hand side of the bulletin board. There was an alert for tomorrow, and it looked like everybody was going. This, I assumed, is what they meant by a "Maximum Effort."

We hit the sack early, but I didn't go to sleep for a long time. I lay in my bunk mentally reliving today's mission, trying to remember in more detail what it had been like. Did I really have a problem with my oxygen supply, or was it just my imagination? I guess I was trying to get mentally prepared to start the whole thing again a few hours from now. I finally drifted off to sleep. But not for long.

When the lights came on I looked at my watch and it wasn't quite two-thirty. Damn, why so early? The guy with the clipboard was rattling off names and reciting the times for breakfast and briefing. His last comment was, "Fuel load 2,780." While I was dressing and getting fully awake, I remembered that 2,780 gallons of gasoline is all a B-17 could hold, so I surmised that we weren't going just across the Channel today.

We walked out of the hut into a pitch-black morning that was cool and damp. I knew it was foggy. I couldn't see the fog, but I could feel it. We had fresh eggs and bacon for breakfast. The day before we'd had powdered eggs and Spam. I wondered idly if this was another indication about today's mission. A full fuel load, fresh eggs for breakfast; maybe they were planning something extra special for us today.

Briefing was lengthy and filled with details about the weather, the importance of the target, what to do if we had to bail out, and the likelihood of German fighter attacks. I listened, but didn't really hear anything except that we were going to Hamburg and the flak was expected to be "intense." The day before I think the G-2 Officer had said the flak would be "meager to moderate." It turned out to be meager. But today he seemed very sure it would be intense.

While I was suiting up in the Equipment Room, I remembered that our target was a big synthetic oil refinery. I also remembered some of the veterans talking about the oil industry targets as being the roughest kind.

We got off the runway, using almost all of the concrete strip, and climbed slowly into the dark fog. I looked at my watch when we broke out into clear sky. The sun would be coming up soon. It was four-thirty.

We spent the next hour climbing and circling, climbing and circling, forming up the Group. Finally we headed northeast and in a few minutes I could see the North Sea below us. We droned on over this unfriendly, menacing ocean until nine o'clock, then made a shallow right turn. Our altitude was just over 25,000 feet, and it was bitterly cold. My "blue bunny" heated suit under my flight coveralls was doing its best to keep me warm. It was hot where the suit pressed tight against my body, and cold in the spots where it didn't. Occasionally I pressed the suit against my cold stomach, to feel the warmth for a little while.

We made a sharp right turn and the pilot announced we were coming up on the I.P. Our bomb run was north to south, right over the heart of Hamburg. The oil refinery was at Harburg, on the southern edge of the city. The flak bursts started by the time we levelled out on the bomb run, and as we flew along in what seemed like slow-motion, the bursts got closer to us, more frequent, and closer together. In five minutes or so there were ugly black splotches everywhere I looked.

A flak burst starts as a greasy, opaque black, then blossoms into a vertical hourglass shape. As it forms, it changes from black to a dark charcoal-gray color. And then our plane swept past it and it was gone, replaced by another, and another, and another. The really close bursts started out as a bright red fireball for just an instant, then blossomed into the black, ugly flower. These were frequently followed by the sound of metal against metal, as the fragments ripped through the aluminum skin of our airplane.

For the first time I realized how vulnerable we were on the bomb run. We plowed along, slowly, bomb bay doors open, in an absolutely unwavering straight line, and no variation in altitude or course. To bomb properly, a B-17 made itself a perfect target. That's the way it had to be, I knew that. But I didn't like it.

The bomb run seemed to last forever; actually, it was probably about fifteen minutes. Then it was over, we were banking sharply to the right out of the target area, and the flak stopped almost immediately. I could feel the tension drain out of me like a physical thing.

"Look sharp, now—watch for fighters."

"Everybody OK?"

"Damn, look at the smoke down there."

"Yeah, we sure as hell set some fires, didn't we?"

"Knock off the chatter on the intercom!"

Our tires squealed on the runway at twelve-thirty. We had flown for just about eight hours. At Interrogation we sipped hot coffee and straight whiskey and poured out all the details we could think of. We'd lost one plane today. A B-17 from the 407th took a direct hit and went down in a steep dive toward Hamburg. I didn't see it. It wasn't clear whether anybody saw any parachutes.

The Hamburg raid set a new record for the Ninety-second: the most planes ever over a German target. The Group put up fifty B-17s, lost one, and thirty were damaged by flak. I had seen for myself today that a man could definitely get killed doing this.

Back at the hut I sat down on my bunk and at once reached for my little book. I did this unconsciously, without thinking about it, and opened it to the "missions" page . . . "2—June 20—Hamburg."

I thought about what to write on the left-hand page about today's mission. I couldn't think of anything important, and finally closed the book and put it away.

At this point it occurred to me, even after two missions, that this ritual of logging each mission immediately was becoming a fixation, or perhaps a superstition. I didn't think of myself as being superstitious, but I suppose we *all* were, to some extent. Moore had vowed to wear the same pair of trousers on every mission. They were his "lucky" pants, and he hung them separately from the rest of his uniforms, and wore them just on missions. He said he wasn't going to have them cleaned and pressed until he finished his tour.

There was an Alert for the twenty-first, but we weren't on it. I was just as happy to have a day off. Two missions in two days made the two days seem like one long, forty-eight-hour day. Whether the flying time was four hours or eight hours, a mission took all day. The ritual of breakfast, briefing, suiting up, waiting for a truck to the hardstand, pre-flighting the plane, waiting for the flare signal to go, waiting in the taxi-line for our turn on the runway, waiting for the Group to form up. The Air Corps was the same in combat as it was in Training Command, "hurry up and wait."

Wednesday morning nobody came into our hut and turned on the lights. We slept in until seven o'clock, then meandered down to get a shower and shave. The combat mess was still open and we went in. I just intended to have coffee, but wound up with a big plate of "S.O.S." I wondered if I was the only guy in the squadron that liked the "creamed beef on toast," known by a more familiar but less appetizing name. Our breakfast conversation was mostly about where the Group had gone today.

After breakfast we walked around the base for a while, just getting the feel of the place. Everything was spread out, or "dispersed" in military terminology, and it was hard to get a picture of the base as a whole. The barracks area was just across the road from the administrative buildings. Down the road toward the runways was the fuel storage area, and just beyond that hangar number one. The hangar, a big Type T-2 painted flat black, was the most substantial looking building on the base. A few hundred feet beyond it was the control tower, and beyond that the network of runways surrounded by the perimeter track that connected the runways to the widely scattered hardstands. There didn't seem to be many B-17s left on the hardstands. And nobody was hanging around the control tower, so I decided the Group wasn't due back for awhile.

"Let's find out when they're due back and watch them come in." This from the irrepressible Moore. Nobody agreed or disagreed, and we wandered back and stopped in the PX. There wasn't much merchandise, just the necessities. Cigarettes were rationed, and combat personnel got a much bigger ration than ground crews. I didn't think this was fair, but since I was combat crew I decided not to complain.

Back in the barracks area, we heard that a guy we all knew had quit flying. He was an engineer/top turret gunner on a crew we had come over on the boat with, and lived in the Quonset next to ours. He was about twenty-five years old, and I knew he was married and had a couple of kids. His home was in upstate New York. Apparently the Hamburg raid yesterday convinced him that he didn't want to get shot at any more, so he just said he refused to go on any more missions. We discussed this in a wary sort of way, as if it might happen to one of us.

"What do you suppose they'll do to him?"

"Probably bust him to private. Maybe court-martial him."

"I don't think so. I heard that anybody that quits is put on permanent K.P."

I wondered if they would publicly strip him of his rank and maybe tear off his buttons. We all knew he'd be a leper in the squadron. I wondered how he was feeling right now. Maybe they ought to transfer him out.

We spent most of the afternoon in the hut. I was writing a letter when I heard the Group coming back from today's mission. The distant drone of engines quickly became a roar as the first squadron came over the base. We ran outside and watched the big silver planes make a wide turn. The low element peeled off and lined up with the runway, one behind the other. The big white "B" in the black triangle stood out sharply against the red stripe across the fin and rudder.

"Boy, they're beautiful, aren't they?"

"Yeah. Wonder where they went today."

"Look—that one fired a red flare. That means wounded aboard, doesn't it?"

"I think so—or maybe some problem with the plane."

"Sure as hell they went to Germany again!"

And sure as hell they had been to Germany—Berlin, to be exact. It was a Group Maximum Effort, but only thirty-seven B-17s went to Berlin from the Ninety-second. The hammering the flak guns had given us over Hamburg had kept a dozen planes on the ground, with crews working around the clock to get them ready for us to take out and get shot up again.

That night at dinner we learned that we hadn't lost any planes over Berlin. But the way the guys said *Berlin* made it sound like a trip to hell! Every time I heard the word, it was spoken in an ominous-sounding tone. Actually, from what I could hear from the guys on today's mission, it wasn't as bad as Hamburg yesterday. But it was Berlin; "Big B," as one fellow called it. He said, "I was looking right down at the Olympic Stadium when we took a hit in Number Three!" Somebody else said they had a thousand guns protecting the city. That didn't surprise me. What did surprise me was that the Luftwaffe hadn't sent up fighters, at least not against the Ninety-second.

I wasn't alerted for the twenty-second, and decided to check out Rushden. Several of us wanted to buy a bicycle, and Moore wanted to see if the new Bing Crosby movie, "Going My Way," might be playing at the theater. He was having a fit to see it.

We had training sessions scheduled for Thursday morning. I went to the "blister" hangar, along with Lewis, for some practice on turrets and procedures. A couple of the guys went to the skeet range. We got together again at lunch in the combat mess and afterward walked over to the squadron office to sign out. We caught a Liberty Run truck, and in a few minutes we were deposited right in the middle of the town of Rushden.

We strolled around town in a group for awhile, looking in shop windows and occasionally going inside. It was a small, rural town; not a picturesque English village like Podington. There were a few old thatch-roofed buildings, but most were just old brick buildings not unlike the downtown section of Waxahachie, Texas. But Rushden wasn't laid out nice and square like my home town. The little narrow streets wound and twisted and meandered in every direction. Still, I decided I liked Rushden; it was a nice little country town. In fact, I hadn't been any place in England that I disliked, except The Wash.

There wasn't much merchandise in the shops and almost everything was rationed. There were small queues of people outside some of the shops, mostly women waiting in line to buy vegetables, meat, or whatever the shop was selling. I saw several brands of English cigarettes behind the counter in one shop, and asked the lady which was the most popular. She said, "American cigarettes are, but you won't find 'em 'ere!" I looked over the various brands and bought a packet of Players' Weights. She seemed surprised that I wanted them, and actually I don't know why I did. I smoked Lucky Strikes, and had plenty. I suppose I just wanted to sample everything English.

I opened the pack and lit a Players, while Hanley asked the lady where we could find a bicycle shop. The cigarette was terrible. It was rolled so tight I could hardly get it lit. We walked up the street in the direction she indicated and after a while located a shop that looked like it might be the one. They didn't believe in putting up large signs; I suppose everybody in Rushden knew where everything was. This shop had just a number and name on a small plaque alongside a big, drab door that needed a coat of paint. We walked inside and it appeared to be a hardware store. And it was much bigger than it looked from outside.

A thin, elderly fellow walked toward us from the back of the shop and asked if he could assist us. Hanley said we wanted to look at some new bicycles. I looked around the shop but didn't see any.

"You chaps from over at Podington, are ye?"

"Yes sir, just got here. Everybody but us seems to have a bike."

"Well, not any bikes being made. The bloody war, you know. Everything goes to the war effort. Don't believe there's been any new bicycles made in two, three year." The old fellow talked on about the nuisance of the war, and how everything was scarce. He was very pleasant, though, and seemed to be sizing us up. I tried to con him a little.

"We're from Texas, sir, and you know we never learned to walk in Texas."

He laughed and said, "Right—you go about on 'orses, I expect!"

We talked for awhile, and he finally said, "All right, lads, just come along this way."

We followed him along to the back left corner of the shop, and he opened a door on the right. I hadn't noticed the door before. He turned on a light switch and led the way down a wooden stairway to the basement. I looked around in disbelief: the whole place was jammed with bicycles, wheels, tires, and parts hanging on the walls!

We spent about an hour looking over the bikes, most of which were secondhand. Some looked almost new, and I finally picked out a black Raleigh three-speed. It had skinny little tires, not at all like the balloon tires on most American bikes, and the brakes were on the handlebars. He told me I'd made a fine choice, and I could have the bike for fifteen pounds. And he'd throw in a pair of pants clips. I had already noticed that these bikes didn't have chain-guards to protect your trouser legs.

While I counted out the money, it dawned on me that I was paying sixty bucks for a bicycle! Well, hell, easy come, easy go.

Hanley had settled on a dark green racing bicycle, with turndown handlebars and a complicated three-sprocket system, with the chain looped around in a double-S figure. I had never seen anything like it. Apparently Hanley had, and he was bargaining with the shop owner while I pushed my bike up the stairs and through the shop. While I waited for Hanley, I took a trial ride along the street and promptly dumped myself over the handlebars. Those hand brakes would take some getting used to. After a few tries, I figured out that I had to put more pressure on the right and less on the left brake. The left was the front-wheel brake, and too much pressure would jackknife the damn thing.

Hanley finally came out, pushing his green machine through the shop door. The old fellow followed him, and after Hanley had practiced a few turns up and down in front of the shop, we thanked him and rode away. He waved and cautioned us, "Remember, keep *left*, Yanks!"

We pedaled down the street, past the old church and around a bend to the right and spotted a pub sign. It said, "Waggon and Horses." There were a dozen or more bicycles parked on the sidewalk on either side of the door. We added ours to the pile and walked inside. It was just twilight, and I wondered if Hanley knew the way back to the base.

The pub was filled with people, noise, and smoke. The lighting was not exactly dim, just erratic. There were light spots and dark spots. About half the people in the pub were wearing American uniforms, all with Eighth Air Force patches on the right shoulder. A few girls, in pairs and threesomes, were sitting at little iron tables, surrounded by Air Corps guys. The men in civilian clothes were, for the most part, in their fifties or sixties, I guessed.

Hanley and I made our way to the bar. The barman finally got around to us and Hanley ordered a mild-and-bitter. While the barman drew his beer, I asked if he had any bottled beer. He set Hanley's pint on the bar and took a small bottle from the back bar.

"Right," he said, "Guinness is in bottles."

I nodded and he opened the bottle and set it on the bar, along with a glass. I declined the glass and took a sip from the bottle. It was fairly cool, and tasted very rich, with a bitter taste, but very different from the mild-and-bitter, which I found a little watery. I decided the Guinness was OK and drifted out among the people in the pub, bottle in hand.

Conversation in the pub was free and easy. There was an atmosphere that is hard to describe, one I can only call a wartime feeling. The people, particularly the Americans, were having fun, but they weren't quite relaxed. There seemed to be a kind of urgency to have fun, as much fun as possible, as quickly as possible. I had experienced this same feeling in the States, particularly in bars full of uniforms in Los Angeles. But it was not nearly so distinct as here. I ordered another Guinness, and another after that. As I talked with people, and watched them drinking, talking, gesturing, I felt a sort of excitement about being here, in a little pub in the English Midlands, a couple of miles from my airbase, in the middle of a world at war. Not a far-away war, but a right-here war. I was enjoying every minute of it.

My enjoyment ceased suddenly. I don't know how many Guinnesses I'd had, and I wasn't drunk by any means, but I wanted to lie down and be sick. Immediately! My face was covered with sweat; I was deathly ill. I vaguely remember a man in an Air Corps uniform asking if I was OK. I shook my head, and I think I told him I needed to go outside. Somehow I got to a back door and found myself on a grassy lawn behind the pub. I walked down the slope a few yards and leaned against a tree. After I got rid of the Guinness, I felt the cool night air on my face. I unbuttoned my tunic, and my shirt was wet with perspiration.

I have no idea how long I stood there, leaning against the tree and watching the patchy clouds in the pale moonlight. The cool air felt good. I tried not to think about the rich taste of the beer. After a while I went back into the pub. The smell of beer was overpowering, but I was past the crisis now. I lit a Lucky and found Hanley standing near the end of the bar. My face must have looked like I felt, because he grinned when he saw me and asked, "How was the Guinness?"

"You think you can find the way back to the base?"

"I think so. You think you can ride your bicycle?"

"Damn, let's get out of here. I can't take the smell much longer."

There were more little rolling hills than I realized there were, and the turns in the winding road were hard to negotiate in the dark, but we made it back to the base.

I took off my shoes and tunic, pushed the pillow off the bunk, and went to sleep on my stomach. My last thought was, Never again!

FOUR

TURNING POINT

On June 24 the day started early. It was three in the morning when the lights came on in the hut. I heard the guy with the clipboard calling names and giving information, but I was just half-listening. I rolled out of the sack and sat on the edge for a few minutes. After I lit a cigarette and stood up, I realized that I felt different, somehow. No dread, no tightness in the stomach. Not yet anyway.

We shuffled along through the cool darkness toward the combat Mess. Conversation was intermittent; not questions or answers, just muttered comments.

"Full fuel load again."

"Yeah, Germany sure as hell."

"I'd sure like to get a pass to London."

"I'd like to get a mission to France!"

We left the mess hall in ones and twos and walked to the briefing room. Two MPs guarded the door, one of them with a clipboard and a penlight, checking off names to be sure nobody got in who wasn't authorized to be there.

Briefing was like a three-act play. There was a raised stage at the front of the room. On the left was a blackboard sitting on a tripod, and on the right was the big map of Europe. It was covered with a gray curtain. The actors consisted of the Group C.O., the squadron C.O.'s, the G-2 (Intelligence) officer, the station weather officer, and the P.W. (Escape and evasion) officer. The G-2 and the weather officer had most of the lines.

After a brief greeting by the C.O., G-2 got right to the business at hand: he pulled back the curtain from the map. There wasn't a sound in the room. He said, "Today you will attack the oil refinery and storage depot at Bremen," and gave that spot on the map a tap with his pointer. He then turned toward us, standing at a kind of "parade rest" position, and told us about the target, expected enemy resistance, places to avoid while flying to or from the target. He emphasized his speech by tapping the map occasionally with the pointer.

The weather officer gave a detailed report on conditions over England, the North Sea, the target, and what the weather conditions were expected to be when we returned. Today we should be able to bomb visually.

The P.W. officer talked about escape routes in the event we had to bail out. The assumption was that we could parachute to the ground without being spotted and then outmaneuver the Germans who would be looking for us. I had the feeling that if I ever had to bail out I was going to be captured and sent to a Stalag Luft somewhere.

I wondered if the flak at Bremen would be as bad as at Hamburg. That was an oil refinery too, and they really put up a hell of a barrage.

The last thing we did was synchronize our watches. One of the briefing officers said, "Hack your watches—coming up on 0448 in-twenty seconds—ten—five—four—three—two—one—*hack*!" So far, the only reason I'd looked at my wrist watch was when I wanted to know what time it was. But there were specific times to start engines, to taxi, and so on, so I suppose it was best if everybody had exactly the same time.

I got a pleasant surprise in the equipment room. I was issued a new type of heated suit. The old-type "blue bunny" suit was a heavy, one-piece felt coverall that was stiff as a board, and when I put it on and wrestled my flight coveralls over it, I moved like Frankenstein's monster. This one was a two-piece green nylon, interlaced with electric heating wires. The jacket and pants plugged in together, and the whole thing was lightweight and comfortable. My flight coveralls slipped on easily over this, and I found I could actually move, and bend, and walk.

We got off the ground while it was still dark and slowly climbed out of the layer of mist and patchy fog. Then the long process of "forming up" began; circling, climbing, watching for our Group's flare signal from the lead plane. We finally headed out over the North Sea, flying in tight squadron formation and still climbing. We were at 25,000 feet when we passed the Frisian Islands. I could barely see them off to our right. About fifteen minutes later we made a slow turn to the right. Almost the same route as the mission to Hamburg, I thought, and my stomach started to tighten up. By the time the pilot announced that we were turning on the I.P., I felt the tenseness building up. The expression about "butterflies in the stomach" was actually very appropriate. I had a sort of jittery feeling like an empty stomach, but I wasn't nervous. My hands were steady, even when I saw the first flak bursts. As we got into the flak, I was scared, no question about it. Every muscle was tense, and I couldn't get them to relax. But I realized I wasn't petrified, as I had been on the first two missions.

Suddenly I was hitting the toggle switch, then the door lever, and we were banking out of the target area. Out of the flak. I tried to tell myself that it wasn't so bad; moderate, maybe, but not intense. Then it dawned on me how ridiculous this was. After only three missions, I was an expert on flak.

We didn't lose any B-17s over Bremen, and battle damage wasn't as bad as Hamburg. When I sat down on the edge of my bunk and faithfully recorded the mission, I thought about making a comment on the left-hand page. Something about my confidence in what I'm doing; something like that. I finally decided not to. Better give it a couple more tries before I start feeling like I've got it made. There are still a lot of blank lines to be filled in. Twenty-seven more, to be exact.

The thirty-mission tour had been set early in the year, long before I arrived. Originally a tour was twenty-five, back in the days before long-range fighters escorted us all the way to the target. In those days the fighters escorted the B-17s as far as they could, then when their fuel got low they peeled off and headed back to England. From then on the bombers had to slug it out with the Messerschmitts by themselves, and the chances of completing twenty-five missions weren't too good. Still, I reasoned, even an unprotected squadron of B-17s wasn't exactly a bunch of sitting ducks. A B-17 is a tough airplane, hard to shoot down, and equipped to do a hell of a lot of shooting back. It wasn't a one-sided battle. The first raid on Schweinfurt, back in August 1943, that bloody battle with such heavy losses that some people wanted to abandon daylight bombing, inflicted heavy losses on the Luftwaffe as well. The gunners on those 188 B-17s filed claims for 148 German fighters shot down, 18 "probables," and 63 damaged. B-17s were far from helpless, even without a fighter escort. So far I hadn't seen an enemy fighter, but I had seen a hell of a lot of flak. That stuff could do the same thing to a bomber that fighters could do, and quicker.

I wasn't alerted again for several days. The Group flew on the twenty-fifth and twenty-eighth, both times to France, on battle-area support raids. These French raids were considered much less hazardous, and I'd like to have gotten one to add to my score, but they seemed to be saving me for Germany!

Life on the base was fairly relaxed and casual from a military standpoint. We didn't "play soldier" a lot. There were occasional reminders that we *were* in the Army and things like clean shaves, shined shoes, and proper uniform hadn't been abandoned. But most of the official activities when we weren't flying were training sessions directly related to flying.

Life in the hut, with my original crew members, was just as casual and relaxed as if we were still on the same crew. I was happy that we weren't, because I liked my new position in the nose so much better than being in the back of the airplane. I took a little kidding about being a toggle jockey, especially when I left the hut to spend some time down at the bomb trainer. Hanley once suggested I get plenty of "bombardier's exercise," and he flexed his index finger back and forth in the same way you'd flex your biceps.

I spent a good deal of my spare time down at the training building. There were mock-ups of turrets, bombardier's panel, and all the other technical gadgets found in the innards of a B-17. I got to know the bombardier's panel and the chin turret sight and controls so that I could literally operate them blindfolded. I worked on doing everything in the same sequence; I was less likely to screw up that way.

The time we spent in the hut was occupied by catching up on our sack time or writing letters. And at night there was almost inevitably a card game, blackjack or poker, usually for penny-ante stakes. I was addicted to reading, but I did my reading at the Aero Club. The light was better, the big easy chairs more comfortable, and I could always take a break for a beer or a Coke.

Around the base the leather A-2 jacket was the most popular piece of uniform, although it was seldom worn on missions. I got a Squadron insignia and had it sewn on the left breast of my A-2, which added a combat look to the jacket. The 326th insignia pictured Alley Oop on his dinosaur, waving his stone battle-axe in the air, while the dinosaur held a bomb wrapped in his tail. Properly decorated and topped off with a

Insignia of 326th Bomb Squadron.

grommetless fifty-mission-crush cap the outfit maintained the glamorous image I associated with the Air Corps. We didn't look nearly so glamorous when suited up in battle gear for an actual mission.

The radio in our hut and the *Stars and Stripes* newspaper kept us filled in on the progress of the war. There was a great battle raging on the Cherbourg peninsula, with U.S. troops trying to drive out or cut off the German forces holding that area. Our troops had moved a long way from Omaha and Utah beaches where they had landed only three weeks ago. According to the news reports, we were almost to the port of Cherbourg itself. A battle area map in *Stars and Stripes* showed the positions of the various Allied forces, and it seemed to me that the British hadn't moved very far inland. They had landed at Sword, Gold, and Juno beaches to the east of Omaha and Utah, and they didn't seem to have made much progress.

Stars and Stripes gave equal coverage to the air war, and one issue featured a photo of a B-17 on the front page, with an article intended to show how tough and reliable the airplane was. This one had gotten home after being heavily damaged over Germany, bringing its crew safely back to their base. Not quite all the crew, however. The nose of the plane had been blown completely away! In view of where I sat in a B-17, I took very little comfort from that picture.

During my four days of no flying, conversations with various guys in the squadron gave me a better picture of the Ninety-second's role in the overall scheme of things. We were one of three groups that made up the Fortieth Combat Bombardment Wing. The other two were the 305th at Chelveston and the 306th at Thurleigh. These two groups were just a few miles from Podington, east and northeast. I had heard the references to "The Wing" at briefing, and I believe we were the lead group for the Wing on the Hamburg raid. Now I knew what a Wing was: about 150 B-17s, give or take a few.

Conversations were always liberally spiced with flak stories. But I must have heard a dozen guys tell about missions and they all seemed to start out, "There we were at 26,000 over something-burg with one engine on fire—" I took these mostly with a grain of salt. One time, walking to the combat mess with three or four guys, I was chatting with a fellow who mentioned that he had to go by Supply and pick up a new pair of Ray-Ban sunglasses. I asked what happened to his, and he answered in a casual, matter-of-fact way, "Lost them over Cottbus. We took a hit and the airplane went into a flat spin, and I never could find them after that." He said this in the same tone of voice that he might have said, "I sat on them and they broke."

The Alert List posted on June 28 looked like everybody would be going tomorrow. Once again they had shifted from battle-area French targets back to Germany. I was alerted to go, of course.

At three in the morning the sergeant with the clipboard read off names and recited times for breakfast and briefing. He finished with the usual "fuel load 2,780 gallons." Germany, no doubt about it.

My wool shirt and pants felt good. Here it was, almost July, and back in Texas it was probably getting up near a hundred degrees during the day. I knew now why we didn't bring any summer uniforms to England. While I was getting dressed I thought about how much gasoline we were going to use today. I hadn't realized until a week or so ago that the wing of a B-17 was one huge gas tank. There were rubber cells inside, full of high-octane gasoline. Somebody said they extended out to within eighteen inches of each wingtip. The cells were supposed to be self-sealing if punctured, but if a flak burst was close, or even worse, *inside* the wing. . .

We walked out into another cool, dark morning, and I could feel that it was foggy. I couldn't see it, because there was no light to illuminate the gray, swirling mist, but I knew it was there. We stumbled along in the dark toward the combat mess, bitching about everything in general. I mentioned my theory that if we had fresh eggs this morning, we were going on a long trip to Germany. Nobody agreed or disagreed. We had fresh eggs and Spam for breakfast. My appetite was good, even with the funny feeling in my stomach. That was just as well, because there was no food available on a B-17, unless you count the candy bars.

When G-2 pulled the curtain for briefing, the red yarn ran just where I expected, deep into Germany. A big city, I could see from the map, somewhere in southeast Germany.

"Today the First Division will attack major strategic targets in the Leipzig area. We are assigned the Luftwaffe airbase at Quackenbruck. Other groups will attack aircraft-parts factories, the ball bearing plant, and the synthetic oil refinery at Bohlen."

I listened intently, and realized that I was actually interested in what he was saying. At the first three briefings I attended, all I heard was the target and the amount of flak expected. "Your route will take you over the Dutch coast at Schouwen—here—" he tapped the map with his pointer—"then across the German border north of Münster—south of Hannover—here—at an altitude of 25,000."

As we left the briefing room I heard somebody say, "If the Luftwaffe won't come to us, we'll go to them." I hoped silently that our attack on their airfield would probably keep them on the ground instead of luring them up after us. I imagined that the P-51 pilots escorting us would like them to come up. My mental image of a fighter jockey was that he wanted to be an ace, and escorting bombers was probably dull business. Maybe not; flak got P-51s the same as it got B-17s. But then they didn't have to fly straight through it. They could zoom around as they pleased, so long as they stayed close enough to our formation to give us moral support.

The trip to Leipzig was a long, long haul. The jittery feeling in my stomach didn't keep me from watching everything, and I tried my hand at navigating. Jack was a "Mickey" navigator, and he stayed glued to his little "G-box" radar scope above his table. I borrowed one of his maps and leaned forward in the nose as we approached the Dutch coast. I spotted the island of Schouwen, and one called Overflakkee.

"Pilot to crew, crossing the Dutch coast—look sharp."

A little after that I called for an oxygen check. The crew responded with OKs from tail to front. I went back to my imagined navigating, occasionally scanning the sky and spotting other groups of B-17s leaving stark white contrails in the dark blue sky. What a hell of a sight we made; I wondered why I hadn't realized it before. My fascination with what I was seeing was occasionally interrupted by thoughts of what we were going to do, and the tingling "empty stomach" feeling returned. But today I felt a kind of exhilaration that hadn't been there before.

The closer we got to Leipzig, the more often the tingling feeling came back. About twenty minutes before the I.P. the pilot suggested we get into our flak suits. Jack and I assisted one another and were enclosed in our portable foxholes by the time we got to the I.P. As we made our turn, I pulled my goggles down over my oxygen mask so I could see more clearly. My eyes were glued on the lead plane. The instant I saw his bomb bay doors start to open I hit my lever and called out, "Bomb bay doors open!"

I got a "Roger" from the radio operator, and started turning on all the switches. The flak started while I was getting everything ready to relieve us of 6,000 pounds of high explosives. The bomb run was long and steady, almost in slow-motion. Then in a matter of seconds it was all over. I hit the toggle switch, the B-17 bucked upward, there were rapid-fire exchanges on the intercom, and we were banking away from Leipzig.

There was still a little flak following us when I leaned all the way into the Plexiglas nose and tried to see our bomb strike on the ground. I saw several areas of bomb-bursts and smoke, probably ours and some other groups'. Then it occurred to me that I'd better start watching for fighters. We had just bombed a Luftwaffe base.

The only fighters I saw were four beautiful silver P-51s that slid over us from right to left, pulling ahead and away from our formation. We were still turning and I lost sight of them. The flak had stopped now, and I called for an oxygen check.

The long trip back out of Germany and across Holland, the Channel, and half of England was pleasantly boring.

The Group was on stand-down the last day of June. The Leipzig raid on the twenty-ninth was a kind of turning point for me. I felt like I had things under control. I felt like a combat flyer.

Posted on the bulletin board in the squadron office was a commendation from General Doolittle and General Spaatz about the mission to Hamburg ten days ago: "Operations 20 June 1944 against difficult targets in Germany considered among most satisfactory ever conducted. You are congratulated for these successes." But more interesting, I thought, was a postscript about yesterday's raid on Leipzig. The Eighth Fighter Command claimed fifty German fighters destroyed and seventeen damaged. Apparently the Luftwaffe wasn't dead yet. I hadn't seen a single German fighter so far, but somebody had spotted some around Leipzig yesterday.

With four missions behind me, three of them to German targets, I had begun to feel that I could handle combat flying. Before my first mission I wondered what I'd do under fire. The first two missions didn't satisfactorily provide an answer to the question. But then, over Bremen, I found that I was beginning to settle down. The Leipzig raid convinced me that I could stop worrying about it. The knot in my stomach, and the fear when we flew into a flak barrage would still be there. I had no doubt about that. But any doubts about whether I could function properly under fire were gone.

FIVE

LONDON

The train crept forward, sometimes stopping completely, then inching ahead tentatively through the maze of tracks. I gazed intently through the window, trying not to miss anything. I had been glued to the window for almost two hours, ever since we left Wellingborough station. An hour earlier we were speeding through the English Midlands, and the view from the train window was a panorama of tidy farms, stone fences, grazing sheep, and the lush greenery of England in summer. Occasionally we passed a town or village—picturesque, typically English towns, each with its tall, slender church spire.

Since our last stop at Luton, however, I had noticed a decided change in scenery. Luton was not like the rural cities; it was about the same size as Bedford, where we had stopped earlier, but Luton had a more "industrial" look about it. I could see factories, warehouses, and tall chimneys emitting gray smoke that hung almost still in the summer sky. And now, half an hour later, we were crawling through a sea of buildings, warehouses, huge storage tanks, freight cars, all covered with a thick layer of soot. I could see grimy trucks moving their cargo from one place to another, and men in dirty workclothes working on the tracks, or unloading freight cars. This had to be London, but it wasn't the way I had pictured it.

I thought about how many cities I had seen for the first time through the window of a train: Los Angeles, Denver, Chicago, Boston. It was a poor way to form a first impression of a city. It seemed as if the railroad tracks were deliberately planned to take you through the ugliest part of the city. Coming into London was no different. The clear summer air of the rural Midlands was replaced by a bluish haze of smoke and cinders that seemed to permeate the air.

There were four others in the little compartment: Lester, Hanley, Horton, and Moore. Today was the Fourth of July, 1944, and we all thought it was an appropriate day to visit London for the first time. I was as excited as a kid going to the circus, and I think the others were too.

Maybe not Hanley, however; he was older and much more worldly than the rest of us. He sat there smiling, looking from one of us to the other, and seemed to be enjoying our excitement more than the prospect of two days in London.

The ugly industrial area gradually gave way to an ugly residential area. There were still occasional warehouses or factories, but pushed tightly together in between were sooty brick buildings where people lived. The grimy slate roofs blossomed with chimney pots, and clotheslines strung across back porches blossomed with shirts and pants and baby diapers hung out to dry in the sooty summer air. I unhooked the leather strap from the bottom of the compartment window and lowered the window. Leaning out, I could see that the train was going inside a building, a really big building.

"Hey, guys, I think we're coming into the station."

We got up and collected our possessions from the overhead rack. Each of us carried a khaki canvas musette bag stuffed with shirts, socks, underwear, and cigarettes. While the train eased into the station I sat back on the seat and looked around our little compartment. It reminded me of the inside of a stagecoach in a western movie. The bench seats across the front and back of the compartment were oak, well worn and covered with faded blue velour. Ornate lights were mounted on the wall on either side. Victorian, I assumed. And finally there was the leather strap to raise or lower the window then secure it by hooking the strap over a brass stud. Old. Everything in England seemed to be old.

We stepped onto the platform and started walking toward the front of the train, gawking at the enormous size of St. Pancras station. I looked up at the roof, a giant checkerboard of iron that at one time was filled with glass panes. I knew why the glass had been removed: the blitz. I estimated the distance from the platform to the roof to be about a hundred feet.

When we were past the front of the train I could see six or seven other trains in the station and platforms to accommodate even more. We stopped to ask a fellow wearing an LMS Railway uniform where we could find a taxi. He said something completely unintelligible and pointed toward the right front of the station. We thanked him and headed in the direction he pointed.

"Did you understand what he said?"

"Not a word. I think he must be a cockney."

As we walked across the huge waiting room, I realized why London had so many railway stations. Each station was a dead end, terminating in London. So the rail lines must fan out in different directions, going to different parts of England. Depending on where you're going, you have to know which station to leave from.

Past the booking windows, each with a queue of people waiting to buy tickets, I saw an opening and spotted an occasional little black taxi scooting past. We walked outside and the lead taxi peeled off and arrived at the curb about the same time we did. We jammed inside and I was surprised at the amount of room in the back.

The driver asked where we'd like to go. He was a lean old fellow with a weathered face, probably fifty or older. When we didn't answer immediately, he said, "Wantin' an 'otel, are ye?"

Hanley said, "Do you think we can get rooms at the Regent Palace?"

I wondered where he'd heard of the Regent Palace. I knew he hadn't been here before.

"Don't know if they're booked up or not, lads, but we can give 'er a go. Right near Piccadilly, it is, and lots of other 'otels in that part o' the city."

It took about twenty-five minutes to get to the hotel. We wound through some of the narrowest streets I'd ever seen, in some places no wider than sidewalks. On both sides were buildings, wall to wall. It was like driving through a canyon; we were too close to the buildings to get a good overall view. Just fleeting glimpses of entrances with big ornate doorways in the endless line of brick and stone buildings. I couldn't make out whether they were shops, offices, apartments, pubs, or what. But they were old, no doubt about that. Old and sort of neglected; the brick needed cleaning and the doors and window frames needed a new coat of paint.

I had expected to see whole blocks of bombed-out buildings. This was the city the Luftwaffe had tried so hard to destroy, sending masses of bombers night after night. I remembered Edward R. Murrow's broadcasts describing the fires raging in hundreds of places, and buildings collapsing. During one broadcast he said that there were ten thousand fire engines working in London, in a single night. And now the buzz-bomb blitz was at its height. The little jet-powered doodlebugs, each carrying a ton of explosives, were being launched from Calais day and night. But except for occasional boarded-up spaces where there used to be buildings, there was no evidence that London was virtually destroyed. Maybe this part of London wasn't bombed a lot. Or maybe London was just so damn big that it was impossible to destroy it. I remembered Murrow saying on one of his broadcasts during the blitz, "What a puny effort is this, to destroy a great city!"

No, London wasn't in ruins. Not by any means. But there was a feeling of war, a look of war about the city.

As we got closer to Piccadilly the traffic increased until we were threading our way through a sea of people, walking or riding bicycles. Taxis, buses, cars were jammed into the little streets. We were out of the canyons of unidentifiable brick buildings, and now we passed tree-covered parks with walkways and benches, blocks of shops and hotels. We were in downtown London now, and it was more the way I had envisioned it.

The taxi stopped suddenly, about six inches behind another taxi parked at the curb.

"Well, 'ere we are, lads. If they can't accommodate ye, I'm sure they'll put you onto another 'otel."

We took a while figuring out the pounds and shillings and pence, and gave the taxi driver a tip that I thought was probably larger than the fare. None of us had figured out the English monetary system, and we customarily held out a handful of various currency and coins and said, "Just take what you want."

The lobby of the hotel was elegant, with ornate crystal chandeliers and marble floors. We queued up in a line of five or six people working their way toward an imposing counter with a sign that said "Receptions." Finally it was our turn at the counter. The receptions clerk said she could give us two rooms, adjoining, with a bath in between. We didn't even ask how much; we had plenty of money, and we hadn't had a chance to spend it, except for buying the bicycles.

The rooms were smaller than I had expected, but nice. I could see that they had once been very elegant, but could use new carpeting and curtains. A coat of paint wouldn't hurt, either. But no doubt all would go unpainted and unrefurbished until the war was won.

We sorted out who was going to be where, and Lester and I wound up in the smaller room with twin beds, the other three in the room with a double bed and a twin. I dumped my musette bag on a bed and went through the bathroom, where Horton and Moore were washing up. I went on into their room and saw Hanley sitting on the bed, staring at the window. He had an unlit cigarette in his mouth and a Zippo lighter in his hand, and was absolutely motionless. I asked him what was going on, but he didn't move. Finally he pointed to the window and said, "I just saw a buzz bomb coming straight at that window!"

"The hell you did!"

"The hell I didn't. It looked like it was coming right into the damn room!"

He walked over to the window and looked out. The others came in and he recounted the sight of a buzz bomb coming straight at him. We didn't doubt that he saw it; it must have passed over the hotel and exploded somewhere else. Hanley was calmed down now, and lit his cigarette. "Let's go get a drink. I could use one."

It took only a few minutes and a short walk to locate the American Bar. It was just off Piccadilly Circus, and looked like it had been there for years. I wondered if it had been renamed since the war started, to make it more appealing to our servicemen. It was a nice place, somewhat posh, and looked more like an American bar than an English pub. We sat and drank for about an hour, learning several things in the process. "Whisky" was Scotch; there was no bourbon. Drinks had no ice in them, but you could request it. After a couple of whiskies, the waiter said there was no more, and we switched to gin. You could have it straight, and it tasted like perfume, or you could have it with orange or lemon squash, which I didn't care for. After a while we all were drinking the familiar pints of mild-and-bitter.

We drank right through the lunch hour, but nobody was ready to eat, so we walked until we came to Trafalgar Square. I was awed by the tall stone pedestal, topped with the statue of Lord Nelson, and the immense bronze lions that guarded it. The square was filled with people and pigeons. A sidewalk photographer talked us into having a picture made, and we lined up in a stiff pose for the camera. He did the prints right there, and charged us ten shillings each. We asked him where Buckingham Palace was and he gave us directions.

We were just a few yards from Trafalgar when a curbside taxi driver, leaning against his taxi, asked, "Would you Yanks like a tour of London?" We looked at one another and after a few "Whaddaya think?" and "Fine with me," remarks, we decided it might be a good idea. It was a smart decision. The taxi had a fold-down top, and it was a nice July day, so we sat back and enjoyed a grand tour of London. The driver took us everywhere—Buckingham Palace, St. James's, Westminster Abbey, Parliament, St. Paul's Cathedral. He even took us to the docks to see the terrible bomb damage, and all the while he gave us a running commentary that included the history of the city. He seemed to be enjoying the tour as much as we were, and he was in no hurry. We went inside most of the famous buildings and he conducted us on a tour of the interiors.

Inside one building he pointed out a statue of General Cornwallis. We began to kid him about today being the Fourth of July. He was good natured about it, and had the last word, "Well, the General got this 'ere statue, you chaps got your country, so everybody's 'appy, right?" I thought that was damn well put, and we didn't bring up the Fourth for the rest of the day. Back at Trafalgar Square, we paid the cabbie and offered to buy him a drink. He thanked us, but declined, saying, "I've got the night ahead of me, and London in the blackout is no picnic, even wi' a clear 'ead!"

Everybody I had met in England was courteous, if not cordial, and everything I'd seen was fascinating. I wondered why a lot of the guys in the Group bitched so much about England and the English.

We had dinner at the hotel. It was almost eight o'clock, and I'd had no lunch, four or five drinks, two or three pints of beer, yet I was cold sober. It was the excitement of the day, I suppose. After dinner we went up to the rooms and sat around on the beds talking about London. We agreed that as soon as it was good and dark we wanted to head for Piccadilly Circus. We'd heard a lot about the infamous Piccadilly Commandos and wanted to see them up close. I tried to imagine what it was like in a city so enormous as London in total blackout.

When we left the hotel and walked toward Piccadilly it was almost dark. The atmosphere was totally different, sort of eerie. An occasional taxi crept past us, following two little puddles of light made by the slits in the covered headlights. The sidewalks were still filled with people. Most of them used tiny flashlights. Here and there was a little momentary glow as someone flicked on a light to see his watch or look for a number beside a doorway. After a while I noticed that the lights were always aimed downward. Londoners were well-trained. A light shining upward could be seen from the air.

The closer we got to Piccadilly Circus, the more people jammed the sidewalks. I wondered where in hell they were going. For that matter, where were we going?

I lit a cigarette, stepping underneath an arch over a shop doorway before lighting my Zippo. I'd seen other people do this, and I assumed that a naked light would get me an admonition from a bobby. And the bobbies were out in force, sauntering along with their hands clasped behind their backs.

Then I met my first Piccadilly Commando. She bumped into me by accident, or so it seemed. She said, "Sorry, ducks," but didn't move away. And I responded with a corny and unoriginal, "Sure is dark, isn't it?" I could make out her fur coat and blond hair, but couldn't tell what she looked like.

"Care for a cigarette?" That wasn't very original either.

"Don't mind if I do." She stepped over against a building and I offered her a Lucky Strike. She flicked on her penlight as if to find the pack and take a cigarette, but she aimed it more at herself. Her coat was partly open and I could see the tight, short skirt under the coat. She had a great figure. I wondered what her face looked like—in the light of day, preferably. She turned off the penlight and I lighted her cigarette. She had shown me the merchandise in the most casual and innocent way. I figured she'd had a lot of practice.

We chatted for a few minutes in hushed voices. She commented on my wings, and I guessed she knew exactly how much flight pay I made. After a while she apparently decided that I was just window-shopping and we went our separate ways. She never got down to quoting a price, but I understood that it was standard: Five pounds all night, ten shillings for a "quickie."

Lester and I stayed pretty much together. The other guys were lost somewhere in the throngs of people wandering aimlessly around Piccadilly. About midnight we decided to walk back to the Regent Palace to see if the bar was still open. It wasn't, and that was good news to me. I was ready to hit the sack.

We slept late Wednesday morning and still hadn't decided what we wanted to do after we'd showered, shaved, dressed, and had coffee in the hotel dining room. We spent the morning wandering around the Soho area, sightseeing. We had lunch in a nice little restaurant near Marble Arch and decided to split up and do what we each pleased. We agreed to meet at the hotel at four. Our train was to leave from St. Pancras at six-twenty.

Window-shopping along Regent Street I passed a doorway that smelled of leather goods, and walked into the shop. I spent most of an hour browsing, and finally decided I needed a billfold that would fit the pound notes I had crammed into my old one. I finally settled on a dark brown one that felt as creamy as butter. It was compartmentalized and silk lined. "Fine choice," the clerk told me. "It's hand-sewn and fully lined with watered silk." I asked him how much it was, and almost choked when he told me the price, but I bought it anyway.

I wandered on up Regent Street and on to Oxford, and wound up in front of a building with a sign that I recognized. It was a red circle with a blue bar across it that said "Oxford Circus." I had seen these all over London, and found out they were subway stations. The underground was called "The Tube." I'd never been on a subway, so I went in. The ticket was sixpence, and apparently it would take you wherever you wanted to go.

I took the escalator down—way down. Then I walked down some more, down staircases and through broad, cavernous tunnels. The tunnels were lined with tile, and with people. Most of the people weren't taking the train, they *lived there.* The tunnels were jammed along the tiled walls with cots, pallets, suitcases, and people. They were mostly women and kids; some were older men. They looked shabby and grim. I wondered how long they had lived like this; probably ever since the blitz.

A little guy about seven or eight approached me and held out his hand. "Got any gum, chum?" I didn't, but I reached into my pocket and took out some change. "Here, how about a shilling instead?" I was surprised that he didn't want to take it. I insisted I wanted him to have it, and he finally grinned and accepted it. He said, "Ta!" as I walked on toward the platform.

I got on the first train that came by and studied the strip map above the windows. The names were intriguing and completely meaningless to me. I thought I'd go to Tooting-Morden, but it appeared to be the end of the line. I got off at Liverpool Street, for no particular reason.

After walking around for a while, looking at the brown and gray buildings and soaking up the sight and smell and feeling of the city, I decided I wanted to be back where there were shops and pubs and people. There was hardly any traffic here, only an occasional taxi going to or from the railway station alongside the tube entrance. Back on the tube, I studied the strip map and figured out how to get to Piccadilly. I confirmed it by asking a fellow sitting next to me. He said, "Right, get off at Oxford Circus and follow the signs to the Bakerloo platform. You cawn't miss it!" I walked out of the Piccadilly underground station quite pleased with myself.

The pubs in London were elaborate, much larger than the Waggon and Horses in Rushden. I found one called the Red Lion. It had beautiful leaded glass windows across the front and an ornate mahogany and brass doorway. The interior was lavish, with panelled walls, velvet-covered chairs, and polished brass everywhere. There were some people there in uniforms, but most were civilians. I stood at the bar and sipped my pint, chatting with a well-dressed Englishman. He said, after we had talked for a while, that he'd heard a joke and had been anxious to tell it to an American. It involved an American soldier who was complaining to an Englishman about having to be over here. The American said, "Our fathers had to come over here and win the last war, now we're here to win this one. And I guess we'll have to send our children over to win the next one!" The Englishman replied, "Don't bother to send the kids, Yank, just send the bloody uniforms. The kids will already be here!" He thought it was hilarious, but quickly added that he meant no offense. I made a mental note to remember it. It was my first English joke.

We got to St. Pancras an hour before our train time and fought our way through the horde of people into a tea shop in the huge waiting room. We had our tea standing by a narrow shelf along the wall, and spent a half hour just watching people. The little room was jammed; I saw American uniforms, British brown battle dress, RAF blue, and some I couldn't identify. The civilians were a mixture of well-dressed men in suits and hats, working men in grubby clothes and greasy caps, and women in shapeless coats wearing scarves on their heads. I was absolutely fascinated, watching this assortment of humanity. What would London be like if there wasn't a war going on?

During the train ride back to Wellingborough we didn't talk much. I watched the conglomeration of London slide past the window and gradually change into farms and trees and villages. Reflecting on my two days in London, it occurred to me that I hadn't had a date with an English girl. I decided that next time I might come by myself, or maybe with a buddy—but not with four other people.

As we got closer to Wellingborough, I began thinking about whether I'd be alerted to fly tomorrow.

SIX

AIR MEDAL

P ilot to crew, enemy coast coming up. Look sharp!"
　　I leaned forward and peered through the Plexiglas at the hazy outlines four miles below. The Dutch coastal islands were a jumbled, irregular pattern of dull gray. I turned and picked up Jack's map and began to check the shapes of the islands against the shapes on the map. We were coming over Texel, and I could see Vlieland off to the left. After a few minutes we were over the Zuider Zee. Just eight days ago we had flown almost this same route, going to the same place: Leipzig. Two raids in a row, to the same city, seemed odd. As if we had failed to do the job the last time. During briefing I had tried to figure out the logic behind this. From what I could understand it was just a matter of Leipzig having a lot of targets that needed bombing. Eight days ago we had put almost 400 bombers over the city. Today we were going back with just over a thousand heavies! About twenty targets in the Leipzig area were going to catch it today. Ours was a big oil refinery complex called Taucha. I hoped it would be clear over the target so that I would be able to see our hits better than last week when we bombed the airfield. If we really hit the M.P.I. (Mean Point of Impact), which we always seemed to do when Captain Michaelson was the lead bombardier, we should start some fires today for sure.

　　I spotted a river below us that looked like a big one. I checked the map and finally decided it was the Weser. I figured we were just south of Hannover. About an hour and a half to Leipzig, I guessed. "Bombardier to crew. Oxygen check." There hadn't been any conversation on the intercom in a while, so I decided to break the monotony. The crew checked in as usual, in lazy, bored tones. I wondered if I woke some of them up. Their voices would soon sound a lot different, once we got into the flak.

　　There was no problem identifying Leipzig. The party there had already begun. I could see two fields of flak, one straight ahead of us and one off at two o'clock. The smoke markers from a group that had just dropped still showed up clearly, curving down from the flak field to the target. Now it was our turn.

The bomb run always seemed to last for hours. Funny, but I had never timed it. I made a mental note to check my watch at the I.P. on my next mission, and try to remember to check it again at bombs-away. Maybe I would, maybe I wouldn't. What the hell was holding up Michaelson? It *must* be time to drop!

When the moment came I slammed the toggle switch with my left hand and punched the intercom button with my right thumb. My "bombs-away" was more of a scream, my voice sounded too high-pitched in my earphones. When the radioman confirmed that the bombs were gone, I said "Bomb bay doors coming closed" in a calm, matter-of-fact voice. Then I leaned as far forward as I could and peered down to see the strike as we banked out of the target area.

"Tail gunner, can you see the strike?"

"Not yet—Yeah, now, down at four o'clock. Lots of smoke."

I could see it now, gray billows covering a larger and larger area, with thick black smoke starting to build up from three or four places. Storage tanks, probably. I really couldn't see much from five miles up. But I certainly didn't want to be any closer.

After we were off the target and out of the flak, I could feel the fear subside. But the excitement was still there. Doing it again and getting away with it made me almost ecstatic. The adrenaline was still flowing, and I had a cocky grin on my face, hidden under the oxygen mask where nobody could see it.

As far as I was concerned, the mission was over. We were still 600 miles or so from home and there were flak batteries in other places besides Leipzig, but we didn't have to fly over them, straight and level, and pray that none of the stuff hit us personally. All we had to do now was fly out of Germany by the safest route we could find and not be stupid enough to fly over big cities. I should have been more concerned about enemy fighters, because we were constantly reminded that the single-seat fighter was our deadliest adversary, but so far I hadn't seen a fighter except for our P-51s and P-47s. I couldn't believe that a few fighters could do more to harm us than those huge box barrages put up by the flak guns. My main concern was whether I could fly through that stuff twenty-five times more before the law of averages caught up with me.

When our tires squealed on the Podington runway we had been in the air for more than ten hours. The Ninety-second didn't lose any airplanes at Leipzig, which was somewhat surprising, because almost half the B-17s had suffered battle damage. The First Division put 350 Forts over Leipzig, lost seven, and 154 were damaged. The Second and Third Divisions no doubt got the same treatment; they were bombing in the same area. But the Germans took the worst of it. Our bombing was excellent, so maybe we wouldn't have to go back to Leipzig for a while.

The main topic of conversation in the combat mess that night was the death of a gunner from the 327th Squadron. He had died in the base hospital while we were battling our way over Leipzig. The irony of this guy's death was that he had completed his combat tour without a scratch, had been to Berlin five times, and was hit by a jeep while he was bicycling from Rushden back to the base. I was definitely becoming a fatalist, I decided.

The Group flew a mission the next day, July 8, but I wasn't alerted. The mission turned out to be a fiasco, not just for the Ninety-second, but the whole First Division. The weather had turned rotten, and several groups were recalled. Those that did bomb had to find targets of opportunity in that area of France. The Ninety-second found a target of some kind near Prevent, and we lost a B-17 to flak.

The briefing on July 9 was like a battle report on the ground offensive. Our army was fighting its way south, down the Cherbourg Peninsula toward a town called Saint Lô. The First Bomb Division was going to give them an assist by destroying as many bridges as possible, to prevent the German Army from either retreating or bringing up fresh troops.

Two things bothered me about the mission. First, bombing a bridge from high altitude, particularly in an area where there are U.S. troops, seemed like a tricky proposition. Second, and more important, the weather was absolutely lousy. I had decided when I got out of the sack and peeked through the curtain in the hut that we wouldn't be flying today. And at briefing the weather officer said nothing that sounded promising. So we just went through the motions of getting ready for the mission, fully expecting to see the red flare from the tower that signalled the mission was "scrubbed."

We pre-flighted the B-17 on the fog-covered hardstand and sat around for two hours, waiting for the red flare. But damned if they didn't fire a green one.

I couldn't make out the edges of the runway as we roared through the fog, but I leaned forward in the nose and tried to see if we were coming to the end of it. I watched the left landing gear come up into the nacelle and realized we were flying. How in the hell could we bomb a bridge in weather like this? How could we bomb anything, and why did we even take off? I figured that somebody had screwed up and didn't get the word to us.

We finally got formed up and headed over the Channel. I scanned the horizon but couldn't see any other groups, so I began trying to figure out what was below us. There were a few breaks in the clouds, but not many. I finally gave up trying to figure out where we were. I could tell we were changing course frequently, and I supposed we were trying to find a bridge to bomb. I kept my eyes on the lead plane, prepared to do whatever he did. I was resigned to the fact that we would likely get a recall.

But suddenly the lead plane opened his bomb bay doors. I hit the door lever, called it out on the intercom, and we were on the bomb run. Whenever I dared look away from the lead plane, I tried to see what we were attacking, but without success. Then I saw a few flak bursts, well above and ahead of us—just desultory reminders that we were not welcome.

The bomb run was short and sweet, and after bombs-away we flew straight on past the target. I leaned forward and peered through the haze below us. There was a river all right, and a bridge, and as I watched, the whole area began to erupt in a sea of gray bomb bursts. I didn't see the bridge collapse, but as we left the area the whole thing was covered in smoke.

At Interrogation we learned that the bridge was at Chalonnes, and that we had pulverized it. We were one of the few groups to get credit for a mission today. Most were recalled, or wound up salvoing their bombs in the Channel.

Happily I logged number six in my mission log. Another milk run.

Right after our bridge-busting efforts at Chalonnes we got some news from Eighth Air Force Headquarters that was, to say the least, very unwelcome. The combat tour for bomber crews was increased from thirty to thirty-five missions. As far as I could tell, this came as a total surprise to everybody. There had been no rumors about a change in missions, at least none that I had heard.

Bitching was a way of life in the Air Corps. I had heard guys complain about everything from Spam to starched shirts, but this bit of news lifted the art to a new high. The big question seemed to be "What dumb son of a bitch thought this up?" and the best answer was "A goddamned paddlefoot that never got any higher off the ground than his swivel chair!" Some of the guys I talked with, or rather bitched with, had more than twenty missions and this extension really hit them hard. Even with only six, I was already beginning to have thoughts about whether my luck would hold out for twenty-four more. Now make that twenty-*nine* more. I could sense that the guys with only a few to go were sweating them out more than I was.

I was just getting started anyway, so five more probably wouldn't make any difference one way or the other. But I had to have somebody to blame, and I concluded that the culprit was Jimmy Doolittle. He was sort of an Air Corps version of George Patton, and I figured it would be right in character for him to volunteer his dauntless combat crews for additional missions. So I decided that the first five missions were for General Doolittle, and now I had one for myself. As far as I was concerned, my tour was still thirty missions. One down, twenty-nine to go.

We were on stand-down Monday. The weather was still rotten, and I spent most of the day at the Aero Club reading Sherlock Holmes. About mid-afternoon I headed back to the hut to get in a little sack time before dinner. I stopped in the squadron office and joined four other guys going over the Alert list. I found my name, and was checking to see who else was flying tomorrow. It looked like everybody was. A guy standing on my left said, "Hey, Koger, your name's on the hero list."

"What are you talking about?"

"You're getting the Air Medal."

I checked the awards list and found my name, among about forty others. It was no big surprise, I decided, and no big deal. Fly six missions, do what you're supposed to do, stay alive, and you get an Air Medal. Six more and you get an Oak Leaf Cluster. And another, and another. Assuming, of course, that you survive.

My offhand comment about the award—"I'll take a pass to London, and they can keep the Air Medal!"—was the standard reaction, but privately I was very pleased. I looked forward to pinning the blue and orange ribbon underneath my wings. It would move me out of the rookie status. Back at the hut I decided to write a letter home instead of sacking out. It was time to write, and anyway, I wanted to brag a little about getting a medal. I knew my mother and dad would tell everybody in Waxahachie, and probably have it printed in the *Daily Light*.

After dinner we sat around trying to decide whether to play poker, which nobody wanted to do, or go to the base movie. We finally decided on the movie. It was a musical with Danny Kaye, one I had seen back in the States. The newsreel following the movie thoroughly deflated my vanity about the Air Medal. The feature of the film showed an awards ceremony in France. There were about a dozen folding tables lined up, each one stacked with Air Medal cases. I had never seen so many medals—hundreds of them, maybe thousands. Troops were lined up as far as the eye could see, and as they filed past the tables, each hero was handed his Air Medal. It was like a field kitchen handing out K-rations! The narrator explained that these brave soldiers had been dropped into France during the Invasion, some by parachute and some by glider. And every one of them got an Air Medal.

I supposed they deserved them. Anybody who jumped out of an airplane or landed in a glider, which was not really a landing but a "controlled crash," ought to have some recognition. But the sight of those huge stacks of medals certainly diluted the importance of mine. Riding back to the hut after the movie, I wondered if my letter to the folks had sounded too boastful. I wondered if they'd seen that newsreel. I hoped they hadn't.

Returning B-17s taxiing along wintry perimeter track at Podington. Note that inboard propellers are feathered.—*Smithsonian Institution*

Ninety-second Bomb Group crossing the English coast. The three B-17s in the center are the low element of a three-element formation.—*Smithsonian Institution*

Clockwise from top left: Sign at 326th Squadron Area.

Author at age twenty, December 1944.

Checking wind speed on control tower roof just before planes return from a bombing mission.

Passport-size "escape" photograph, showing author in European-style civilian clothing, to be used by Resistance groups to make a fake passport. It was carried on each mission over Europe.

Contrails mark the presence of the Ninety-second Bomb Group high over Germany.—*Smithsonian Institution*

Bomb bays open and flying straight and level, this B-17 makes a perfect target for German gunners five miles below at Ludwigshafen.—*U.S. Air Force*

Five-hundred-pound bombs being wheeled under open bomb bay of a B-17 to be fused and hoisted into position.—*Smithsonian Institution*

B-17s of the 303d Bomb Group drop a load of fragmentation bombs over a German position in France.—*Smithsonian Institution*

B-17 bomb bay, looking forward, showing catwalk.—*Boeing Company Archives*

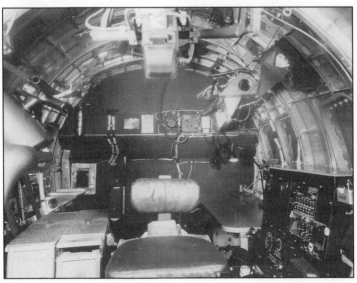

Front seat of B-17, looking in. Optic machine gun sight is visible at top, with bombardier's control panel at lower right. The electric junction box at lower right, marked "452," is the toggle switch used for releasing bombs.—*Boeing Company Archives*

Intense antiaircraft flak over a German oil refinery.—*U.S. Air Force*

B-17s of the Ninety-second en route to a German target, over the Dutch islands at 24,000 feet.—*Smithsonian Institution*

Almost home, a B-17 approaches the English Channel, with all four engines still running.—*Smithsonian Institution*

Crew interrogation after mission. A G-2 officer, shown with back to camera, carefully records each crewman's comments on what he saw and did.—*U.S. Air Force*

HEADQUARTERS NINETY SECOND BOMBARDMENT GROUP(H)
Office of the Group Weather Officer
APO 557

20 June 44

SUBJECT: Interrogation Report on Weather for the Operational Mission by the Ninety Second Bombardment Group (H), on this Date.

MEMO TO: Staff Weather Officer, Hq.1st Bomb.Division,
APO 557, U.S. Army.

1.   Take Off: 0415-0502 hrs. Clouds: Nil high;
nil middle; 9/10 plus L5, base 1000 ft., tops 2300 ft.
Visibility 4 miles.

2.   Route Out: Base to English coast near Louth
to 5425N 0800E to 5402N 1110E to 5336N 1055E to target. The aircraft assembled over the base area at 4000
ft., 5000 ft., and 6000 ft., and departed the base area
at 0528 hrs. The aircraft were within 1000 ft. of 7000
ft. at Louth at 0621 hrs., and climbed to 25000 ft. en-
route. Clouds: 1-3/10 Hl above 28000 ft., nil middle;
9-10/10 L5, base 500-1000 ft., tops 2000-2500 ft. rapidly became nil at 50 miles from the Danish coast. The
eastern edge of the undercast was oriented NE-SW. The
visibility at flight level was unrestricted horizontal-
ly.

3.   Targets: Hamburg and Brunsbuttel, Germany.
Times: 0917 and 0930 hrs. respectively. Height of aircraft: 24000 ft. and 25000 ft. over Hamburg, and 26000
ft. over Brunsbuttel. Temperatures at 24000 ft., 25000
ft., and 26000 ft. respectively: -26 deg.C, -28 deg.C,
and -30 deg.C. Clouds: 2/10 Hl above 28000 ft.; nil middle; and nil low. Downward visibility 40-60 miles.

4.   Return Route: Similar to route out except undercast oriented NE-SW started at 07 deg.E and persisted
to English coast where it broke to 8-10/10 L5, base 1500
ft., tops 2500 ft. and persisted to base.

5. Base on Return: Landed: 1141-1237 hrs. Clouds
9/10 L5, base 1500 ft., tops 2500 ft., nil middle; 1/10
Hl above 28000 ft. Visibility 6 miles.

6.   Remarks: The winds were satisfactory. There
were no contrails.

WILLIAM E. HART
1st Lt.,   AC
Station Weather Officer

Official Weather Interrogation Report for mission to Hamburg, June 20, 1944.

Despite this huge hole made by German antiaircraft fire in the tail assembly of a B-17, this Ninety-second Bomb Group plane made it back to Podington. A mechanic poses in the hole.—*Smithsonian Institution*

This B-17 got back to its base minus its bombardier and navigator, after a direct hit. The chin turret is still in position, attesting to the rigidity of the aircraft.— *Smithsonian Institution*

Left: Captain Erro Michaelson of the 326th Squadron, known throughout the Eighth Air Force for his skill as a lead bombardier.

Right: Sergeant taking temperature reading in front of the Podington control tower, summer 1944.

Visual marker plot, located between control tower and perimeter track, Podington. The symbols tell returning pilots the wind direction and velocity and which runway to use.

The author back in Texas, wearing his thirty-five-mission flight suit.

On a visit to Podington many years later, the author leans against the long-since-abandoned control tower.

Waiting for the London train again after forty years, the author with his wife, Sara, and driver Leighton Price.

The author and his wife with former Luftwaffe General Adolf Galland, October 1980. Galland was interested in the author's encounter with the Me-163 Komet in 1944.

SEVEN

MUNICH WEEK

E ven in the pitch darkness at four o'clock in the morning I could tell that the weather wasn't much improved. There was a chill in the air, and I could smell the dampness. The eleventh of July ought to be warm and balmy, I thought as I groped for my bicycle. Instead it felt like fall back in Texas, perhaps more like winter. I wondered when it was really going to get to be summer in England. Maybe never.

The combat mess was bright and warm and noisy, full of guys not completely awake. Some were bitching, some just muttering about the lousy English weather, and some complaining about the new thirty-five mission tour. By the time I got to the briefing room I was wide awake, as ready to go as I was going to get. I chatted with another bombardier while the briefing room filled up. It seemed like I was always among the first to arrive, as if I were afraid I was going to miss something.

The target today was Munich. The C.O. delivered quite a speech, not just the usual perfunctory remarks. He talked about Munich being the birthplace of the Nazi party, and the vital importance of the city to the German war effort. The entire Eighth Air Force was going to give Munich hell today. It was a pep talk that sounded like a coach getting his team up for the big game.

The G-2 Officer was more specific. Our target was the big central railway marshaling yard. Other groups would bomb the city's main electric power switching station, the BMW motor plant, and a big tire factory. If I understood correctly, the Second Division was attacking the city center together with more than 300 B-24s. That surprised me a little. So far all our targets had been either industrial or military. It didn't bother me, and I knew the RAF was plastering German cities every night, spewing bombs all over the landscape. I was just puzzled, and decided that maybe I had misunderstood. Anyway, we in the Ninety-second Group were going to concentrate on tearing up several miles of railroad tracks.

The briefing finished with our synchronizing our watches, then as usual the bombardiers were excused. We filed out of the room to our own little room adjacent to the big Quonset building. Bombardiers' briefing was a less formal affair. We sat around tables and the G-2 guys passed out maps of the target area, then explained in detail what we were looking at. Then actual photos were passed out, and we pored over these intently, with the G-2 guys showing us what to look for.

I could read the aerial photos only fairly well. Sometimes it was hard for me to see exactly what the guy was talking about, and the Germans camouflaged everything they possibly could. They could make a factory look like a park or an open field. Today I didn't have any trouble; the railway marshaling yards were easily spotted. There were acres of railroad tracks, surrounded by buildings that appeared to be factories or warehouses.

Then we were told it was unlikely that we would see any of this today. The target area would be mostly covered by cloud, and bombing would be PFF, or what we called "Mickey." This British Path Finder Force radar system was almost as good as visual bombing.

We spent some time discussing the bomb load and how to drop it. Today we were carrying twelve 500-pound G.P.—general-purpose, high-explosive—bombs. We would drop by Intervalometer, set for 100-foot spacing on the ground. That made sense to me; walking the bombs along the tracks should foul up the works very satisfactorily. The day before yesterday, when we hit the bridge in France, we salvoed to put all the bombs in the same place.

Our bomb run today would be parallel to the tracks, and this would give us a little crosswind. Normally, we went in with a tail wind. This got us in and out of the target area a little faster, which didn't displease us at all. But a target that was long and narrow, like the marshaling yards, would be damaged much more by flying along its length and spacing the bomb hits from one end to the other.

Bombardiers' briefing only lasted about ten minutes. I was always eager to get out of there and try to beat the pilots and navigators to the equipment room. If we all got there at the same time that place was a mad-house, with everybody pushing and cursing and trying to get all the gear we had to have and put it on. It was very much like a sale in Macy's Bargain Basement—although I had only seen that in the movies.

Munich was about 650 miles, according to my calculations, and there wasn't much to see along the route except the gorgeous topography of the sky. I watched the cloud formations, fascinated by the buildups of tall cumulus. When we passed close by these gigantic white mountains I wished we could fly through some of them. Then I thought about what a shock it would be to see a dozen Messerschmitts come pouring out at us.

I could see groups of bombers in the distance on either side of our formation, some so far away that I could barely make out the white contrails in the soft blue summer sky. I spotted about eight other formations, all seeming to be going the same direction as ours. I wondered how close we'd be to the city before the air raid sirens went off in Munich. Looking at the map I figured the Germans had to know that we were going either to Stuttgart or Munich. And once we passed south of Stuttgart, that would pretty well narrow it down.

About every half-hour I called for an oxygen check. Once in a while somebody else broke the silence and said something routine, usually about spotting a flight of P-51s or another bomb group. One of the gunners treated us to a brief chorus of, "Heigh ho, heigh ho, it's off to work we go!"

We were in our flak suits a long time before we reached the I.P. When we started the bomb run and somebody called the first flak sighting, I noticed that the ball turrets in the other B-17s were spinning madly. I guess they figured that shrapnel might ricochet off a sphere if it were spinning. I wondered if it made them dizzy, whirling like ballerinas through the air.

The lead plane had the PFF dome extended, and it looked like an elongated ball turret with no windows. It took the place of the ball turret, and extended about six feet below the belly of the plane. It was retracted up into the fuselage for takeoff and landing. This Mickey system was being used more and more, and from what I heard the results were about as good as visual bombing with a Norden sight, depending on how good the radar bombardier was.

They shot the hell out of us over Munich. A B-17 from the 407th Squadron took a direct hit over the target and went into the clouds in flames, diving right toward the city. It's a sickening thing to watch a B-17 die. One second it's a sleek, beautiful airplane, sailing along gracefully in its natural element, and an instant later it's a conglomeration of metal and bodies and burning gasoline falling to earth. Curiously, even when a B-17 exploded there were often two or three parachutes seen. I always wondered if those guys actually bailed out, or if they were just blown out and the parachutes popped open.

I tried to concentrate on watching the lead plane and not get so distracted watching the flak bursts. I couldn't help but see it; hell, a lot of it was between me and the lead plane. I couldn't ignore it—but I could try not to focus on it.

Then came the time we were waiting for—the jerk of the plane when the bombs went, the rapid-fire exchanges on the intercom, the steep bank to the right to get the hell away from that place. And the feeling that maybe we'd escaped again.

Munich had been hit hard. The First Division only lost one B-17. Unfortunately it was one of ours. The Ninety-second suffered the only loss in the Division. The Third Division lost three B-17s, but the Second lost sixteen B-24s. I felt for those poor bastards in the B-24s. Somehow that plane was just more vulnerable than the B-17. The facts showed that a B-17 could take more punishment than a B-24 and still stay in the air. I felt much more confident flying B-17s.

The Group was alerted for another Maximum Effort on Wednesday the twelfth, but my name wasn't on the list. I figured it would be a milk run to France. It seemed to be about time for some more battle-area support missions. I was wrong. The Ninety-second went back to Munich on Wednesday. The guys I talked to at dinner that evening said it looked like every bomber in the Eighth was over Munich. I asked about the specific target, and nobody I talked to knew for sure. One guy said, "We were supposed to bomb visually, but there was ten-tenths cloud cover over the place, so we went in PFF—I think we just went for the center of Munich."

"Did we lose any planes?"

"I don't believe so. I didn't see anybody go down, and G-2 didn't say anything about losses at Interrogation."

Two days in a row to Munich. I felt sure that tomorrow would be France, if there was a mission at all.

There was a Mission Alert for Thursday, and I scanned the damn list carefully, but my name wasn't on it. This was beginning to bother me. I was supposed to fly, for Christ's sake, so why didn't they let me?

Thursday afternoon I went down by the control tower and watched the Group land. All the planes got back, and except for a few feathered props they all seemed to be in good shape. As the second squadron was coming in, I turned to a ground crewman standing next to me and asked, "Know where they went today?"

"Yeah, Munich."

"The hell you say! You sure?"

He seemed certain about it, and it turned out he was right. It had been a carbon copy of Wednesday. The intention was to bomb visually, but it was no go, so they went in by PFF. And again, there didn't seem to be any specific target, just the city of Munich. And as on Wednesday, the Group didn't lose any airplanes.

The Group went on stand-down Friday and Saturday. This didn't surprise me a bit. Three days in a row to Munich didn't leave us any airplanes that were fit to fly. I thought about asking for a pass to London, but decided against it. It had only been ten days since my last pass, so I'd try to get in a few more missions before I asked for another one. No sense pushing my luck.

Friday afternoon I signed off the base and bicycled into Rushden with two guys from the hut. We took in a movie at the local cinema and spent a couple of hours afterward at the Waggon and Horses. The pub was jammed tonight; I supposed it was that way when the Group was on stand-down. I noticed that almost everybody in the pub was wearing wings. The ground crews were probably working straight through the night, trying to get the airplanes back on combat-ready status.

The Alert List was posted late Saturday, and I made this one. It had been four days since I flew, and I was getting antsy. Logic told me it was definitely time to shift back to tactical targets in France.

My logic was faulty. An early wake-up, about two-thirty in the morning, told me that we weren't going to France. And briefing told me where we *were* going—back to Munich. The mutter of protest was louder than normal. There was a note of disbelief in the comments—"Come on, they gotta be kidding!" "For Chrissake, have they run out of ideas for targets?" "What the hell's left to bomb there?"

What was left to bomb turned out to be the huge Munich aero engineering factory complex. Half of the First Division was going there, with more than 200 B-17s. The others were targeted for Stuttgart and

Augsburg. And we weren't going to try to bomb visually today. The weather in southern Germany was just too unpredictable. The weather officer mentioned some "unexpected fronts" that had fouled up the missions on Wednesday and Thursday.

We approached Munich at 27,000 feet, flying between huge cloud buildups that rose more than half a mile above us. It was like flying down a valley, surrounded by white mountains. As we got closer to the city, black puffs of flak stood out sharply against the stark white clouds. I watched the box barrage build up in front of us, and decided it was worse than last time. Then I began to hear the flak. It thumped against our plane, and I knew it was tearing holes in the thin aluminum. I had just dropped the bombs when the plane shuddered from a near miss. The plane vibrated for a few seconds, then sort of smoothed out. I looked out the right side and saw that the outboard engine wasn't running. The prop was barely turning, then slowing down, then it stopped suddenly as if it were frozen. The blades were feathered, but I didn't see any smoke.

"Pilot to waist gunner, take a look at number four."

"Roger. It looks OK—no fire, but there's a piece of metal flapping just behind the cowling."

"Roger, waist. We should be able to stay with the formation."

About three hours later we crossed the English coast near Lowestoft, and I was never happier to see England. Off to the left I could make out The Wash, where I had been so miserable a month ago. Was that only a month ago? It seemed more like a year.

We didn't get off lightly today. The Group lost three, one from the 327th Squadron and two from the 325th. Battle damage was extensive. I hoped to hell we were through with Munich.

Apparently we were. The next day we went bridge-busting again, this time to a place called Anizy le Chateau. We bombed visually, hit the Primary, and didn't see much flak. It was about time for a milk run. We were back early in the afternoon, and I got in a couple of hours sack time. On the way back from dinner I checked the Alert List. I didn't think there'd be a mission tomorrow, and if there was, I probably wouldn't be on it.

I was wrong again. There was, and I was. I vowed that I was going to hit the sack early, but in fact we got a blackjack game started and played until almost midnight.

I suppose Munich Week was successful. The city was hit by 800 heavy bombers on the eleventh, more than 1,100 on the twelfth, 500 on the thirteenth, and 200 on the sixteenth. I estimated that something more than 7,000 tons of bombs were dropped, mostly on the city of Munich itself.

The Eighth Air Force lost about sixty-five bombers, and many others must have been damaged. But the city must surely have been left in ruins.

The commendation that General Spaatz sent to the Eighth Air Force after the Munich raids confirmed that we had done what the brass wanted us to do. He congratulated all the crews participating, particularly those who executed the PFF bombing technique, and said that "great damage has been contained in this target area."

The most interesting part of the commendation, to me, was the statement that "These attacks have undoubtedly been severe blows to German war production. They have again shown the people of Munich and all Germany the effective striking power of our Air Forces." I may have been mistaken, but my feeling about the raids on Munich was that we were trying to damage German morale. It's true that we bombed some factories and industrial targets. But the objective, as I saw it, was to put as many tons of bombs on Munich as possible, and show Germany what could be done to their cities by daylight bombers.

I couldn't keep from wondering whether that would work. The Germans did that to London. In fact, they were still doing it. Yet from what I could see, all it did was make the British more determined.

The most important thing about Munich Week to me was that it was over. Maybe the shift back to tactical targets in France would last a while, and I could sneak in a few more easy ones.

The second raid on Munich was unlucky for Lester. He was hit in both legs by flak, and according to the guys on the crew he was really torn up. Apparently all the muscles in his calves were torn and he lost a lot of blood. I hoped to God he didn't lose a leg, or both. I made a promise to visit the big guy with the wide grin and cheer him up if I could, but before I could get over to the base hospital, they transferred him to the big general hospital at Oxford.

Maybe they would give him a Purple Heart and send him back home. At least, I thought, his combat flying days were over.

EIGHT

PEENEMÜNDE

Gentlemen, today you will participate in the first daylight attack on the secret German Rocket Research Center here—at Peenemünde. British Intelligence learned of the activities at Peenemünde through reports of agents in Europe, and recent aerial photographs of the installation indicate beyond a doubt that this is the place where both the V-1 and V-2 weapons were developed. We believe that much of the research is done in underground facilities, but there are surface installations such as the fuel dumps—here—and the production facilities—here and here."

The G-2 officer was popping his pointer against the big map, and what he was saying sounded like something out of a spy movie—secret research, rockets, underground laboratories. Where he was pointing was a long, long way from England, a spot way up on the Baltic coast, almost in Poland. Peering at the map I could see Berlin to the south; Peenemünde was about the same distance. But the way we were going to fly there was not a direct route, and I assumed we would be in the air for well over ten hours.

"Your route to the target will be mostly over water. Across the North Sea past Helgoland to the Danish Corridor. Stay well north of Kiel and Schleswig—here and here. Visibility may not be good over the Corridor, so precise naviagation is important. Be careful not to over-fly Flensburg—here. We believe there are both antiaircraft defenses and fighters in that area. Continue due east over the Baltic, then southeast passing just north of Greifswald—"

I strained to catch every word, to learn everything I could about Peenemünde. I was surprised to learn that the first buzz bombs had been launched against London just barely a month earlier. Now they were sending a couple of hundred a week from the French coast, and London was once again experiencing a blitz. And the V-2 was about ready to be put into action. This was a whole different thing, a rocket that could be launched from anywhere in Germany, lifting a ton of explosive sixty miles high. The V-2 was directed toward London by a highly sophisticated guidance system, and would be travelling at more than twice the speed of sound when it struck London. So there would be no warning of its approach, unlike the V-1 buzz bomb which could be heard several minutes before the engine cut out and it fell to earth.

The briefing officer finished his fascinating commentary by explaining why the V-1 and V-2 were so identified. It seems that Hitler personally named these weapons "Vergeltungswaffen," which translates as "revenge weapons." My head was spinning when I left the briefing room. I felt as if I had just seen an episode from a Buck Rogers movie! I didn't think this would be a particularly easy mission, but it was certainly more interesting than going back to Munich.

We examined the target photos during bombardiers' briefing, and there wasn't a lot to see in the way of reference points. It was a remote and desolate area, and the installations we were attacking were well camouflaged. About the only thing we had to go on was the well-defined shape of the irregular coastline. We could pretty well pinpoint the target in relation to that. We were bombing visually, and Michaelson was leading, so I had no doubt about whether we'd put our bombs on the right spot. Michaelson just never missed.

I squirmed into the nose compartment to pre-flight my area and get things ready, placing my Mae West on the ammo locker and my parachute pack on top of the life jacket. I had gotten into a habit of not wearing the Mae West; it was so damned uncomfortable underneath the parachute harness. My theory was that if I had to bail out, and had time to grab the parachute pack and snap it onto the harness, then I'd also have time to grab the Mae West and take it out the hatch with me when I jumped. This might or might not have worked; fortunately I hadn't had occasion to test it.

Today, though, we were going to be over water for most of the mission, going and coming, probably ten hours in all. I decided that this might be a good day to wear the thing. So I took off the harness and pulled the stiff rubberized life jacket over my head. It covered the chest like an Indian breastplate. I had to readjust my parachute harness to fit over the bulky orange jacket. I finished checking out the compartment and slipped through the hatch to join the rest of the guys. We pulled the props through and hashed over the things we'd heard at briefing while we waited for the green flare from the tower. Everybody seemed excited about where we were going today. I know I sure was. Somebody said, "Maybe we'll take them by surprise, just slip in from the sea, hit them, and slip out again."

"Not likely. Hell, they'll be tracking us over the Corridor for sure - and where else *could* we be going? There's nothing else up there to bomb!"

He was right, I thought, but then the Germans had other worries that day. Almost 1,400 heavy bombers were going out, hitting all over Germany and France. That was a lot of airplanes to keep track of, and even if they did, what could they do about it? Not much, I decided, except put up a lot of flak while we were over the target. For some reason, I wasn't particularly worried about German fighters, because up until now I hadn't seen any.

The flight over the North Sea was like crawling slowly over a never-ending gray cloud deck, with intermittent breaks through which I could see the gray-green water. The barely visible parallel rows of whitecaps verified that we were over water. I spent much of the time idly studying a map of the target area. There were a lot of places with names ending in "munde"—Swinemünde, Warnemünde, Ueckermünde. I knew a little German, so I deduced that since "Mund" meant "mouth," the towns were named for the rivers that emptied into the Baltic.

"Enemy coast coming up." Jack was fiddling with the knobs on his little G-box, watching the bright green images on the tube.

I watched the cloud deck more carefully, and through the breaks I could see land—irregular patterns of gray and brown, not at all like the vivid green patterns of England. I got the map and tried to find where we were, but couldn't. There wasn't anything on the ground that I could see well enough to identify. I did notice one thing: we were over Germany, not Denmark. The Danish border was forty miles north of us; we were over Schleswig-Holstein. While I was musing over the map, the waist gunner called "Flak—flak—nine o'clock" and I dropped the map and ducked. I looked to the left and saw a dozen ugly black puffs with others opening up a little closer to us. We banked sharply to the right and lost a little altitude. The formation got a bit loose, but tightened up again when we straightened out on our due-east course.

"Where the hell did that come from?"

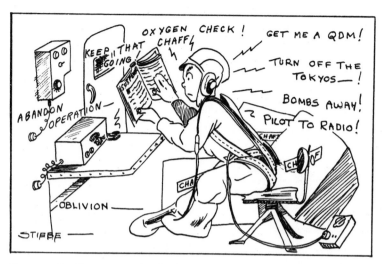

Cartoon of radio operator Art Stiebe at work, drawn by the author after the July 18, 1944, bombing mission to Peenemünde.

"Flensburg—we got a little too close!"

In just minutes we were over water again, and the clouds were thinning out. I could see the streaks of whitecaps, and thought how cold it must be down there. A Mae West wouldn't do much good. It might keep me afloat, but it certainly wouldn't keep me warm. I remembered somebody at one of the briefings saying that a man could only survive for half an hour or so in the North Sea. I assumed that would also apply to the Baltic Sea below us.

I was beginning to think we had taken a wrong heading and were going to fly on into the Arctic Sea or to Never-never land, when we finally made a slow banking turn to the right. Now I could make out the ragged outline of a coastal island that I assumed was Rügen. According to my map we were now over a bay called Greifswalder Bodden. Jack started putting on his flak suit, and I swiveled my seat around to give him a hand. He then helped me with mine, holding the back section up while I fastened the Dzus fittings at the shoulder. I swiveled my seat back to the forward position and tucked the tapered sporran of the flak suit under my crotch. I didn't want an errant piece of flak to hit anything vital.

The bomb run was long, deliberate, and smooth. The target was hard to make out, not because of poor visibility but because it was apparently well camouflaged. It didn't fool Michaelson, though. By the time we made a one-eighty and headed back for the coast, black columns of smoke were rising to 10,000 feet or more. I watched another group of B-17s starting their bomb run, and they appeared to be going for the same target we had just ignited.

The flak over Peenemünde wasn't bad. I wouldn't call it meager, but it was no more than moderate. They didn't put up a typical box barrage, but used tracking fire. The bursts were in groups of four, apparently from synchronized four-gun batteries.

We were well out of the target area when the tail gunner called flak behind us. I wondered where it was coming from. There was nothing below us but open country. We continued to get a few bursts, then it stopped completely and we were over the sea again. I called for an oxygen check, and took off my flak suit while the guys responded on the intercom.

I wondered what it was like to be stationed at Peenemünde. It looked very much like The Wash, from the air, a bleak, desolate place. But according to G-2, most of Germany's top research scientists worked there, underground and safe from our attacks, I assumed. Well, they couldn't have put everything underground, because we left the place in flames. We were well out over the Baltic when I looked back to the left, and I could still see the huge black columns of smoke.

When we lined up at Interrogation to sign for our whiskey I felt like I was still flying. The roar of the engines was still in my ears. I sipped hot coffee and cool Scotch, which seemed to make me more aware of how tired I was. I decided to skip dinner and just sack out as soon as Interrogation was over. Jesus, I hoped I was not alerted for tomorrow. It had been my third day in a row to fly and today was the longest mission ever.

During Interrogation we learned where the late flak was coming from. According to the G-2 officer, the Germans had mounted flak guns on high-speed trains and they sped along our approximate route and popped away at us until we reached the coast. Then they'd pick up a group heading *to* the target and follow them in. He said the trains were almost as fast as our B-17s!

The Group only had thirty-four planes over Peenemünde. It was a Maximum Effort raid, but our aircraft availability was still limited due to the pounding our airplanes had taken in the four trips to Munich. The attack on Peenemünde was rated highly successful and the most important mission we had flown this month. Our efforts elicited commendations from Generals Doolittle, Spaatz, and Williams. General Spaatz called it "One of the finest examples of precision bombing I have seen." The final comment was, "The First Division again demonstrated its ability to destroy the assigned objective regardless of its location or enemy opposition."

I didn't think we had really destroyed it, and enemy opposition was not that bad, although the Division lost three B-17s. But I sure as hell agreed with the part about the location. If it had been any farther away, I don't think we'd have had enough gasoline to get back home.

NINE

DAY AFTER DAY

The day after we paid our respects to the German research efforts at Peenemünde, BBC radio reported that the battle of Saint Lô was over. The commentator referred to it as the "breakout at Saint Lô." I finally got a copy of *Stars and Stripes* and, between the battle reports and the maps, figured out that our troops had broken out of Normandy. Since D-Day they had been fighting up and down the Cherbourg Peninsula, field by field and town by town. Saint Lô appeared to be a fair-sized city, and for several days the troops had been fighting in the streets. Now the Germans were in full retreat, and our guys were ready to pour into Brittany. According to the reports, the Battle of Normandy was over; now, said the BBC commentator, the Battle of France would begin.

I thought that we'd be called on to fly some battle-area support missions, now that the ground offensive was getting up steam. I felt a twinge of guilt about hoping for some nice, easy missions that might come as a result of these guys' efforts. I suppose combat makes a person selfish. I could well imagine what the ground guys were going through—not just occasional scheduled bouts with death, but day in, day out, living in foxholes, wet and dirty and cold. I felt for them, just as I felt for the guys in a B-17 that blew up. But my main concern was my own survival.

The breakthrough at Saint Lô, however, didn't produce any immediate tactical milk runs. I flew another two in a row, both to Germany. On the twentieth we went to Kothen, a small town just north of Leipzig that was unfortunate enough to have an oil storage depot. On the twenty-first we attacked an aircraft parts factory at Ebelsbach. We lost one B-17 over the target at Köthen, and once again we brought our aircraft back with more holes in them than they had when we went out.

I was beginning to feel like an expert on flak. The big targets, like Hamburg and Munich, put up a box barrage, a huge canopy of flak over the city, and we had to fly through it. The Germans' theory, according to

G-2, was that heavy antiaircraft fire would destroy or damage as many bombers as fighters could. In addition, they believed that our bombing accuracy would be noticeably decreased if we had to bomb while under heavy fire. The first part of that theory may have been true, although I had no way of knowing. But the part about heavy fire causing us to bomb inaccurately was surely wrong. I had never seen our formation waver, or shorten a bomb run, or do anything but just plow through the flak, straight and level, as if it didn't exist.

The smaller targets, like Köthen and Ebelsbach, didn't have the hundreds of flak guns necessary to put up a box barrage. Instead they used tracking fire, which could be just as effective. If visibility was good, they could cause us a lot of grief. It was my considered opinion that it was impossible to fly to Germany without being shot at and, in all likelihood, hit. Fortunately, a B-17 can be hit, and hit, and hit, and still fly.

G-2 heightened our "flak phobia" by informing us that Germany had more than *a million people* assigned to flak batteries, more than half inside Germany!

On July 21, while we were making a long trip to a small town, the Second Division sent about 300 B-24s to Munich. To put it mildly, they had a bad day. They lost twenty-two bombers and had 184 damaged, three of those beyond repair. That was even worse than their losses over the same target ten days ago.

The raids on July 20 and 21 involved at least forty German cities. Weather was still a problem. About half the groups couldn't attack their Primary as briefed, and had to fly around looking for targets of opportunity, which was not as satisfactory as it might have been from the Eighth Air Force's standpoint. From the German standpoint, 2,000 heavy bombers dropped something like 5,000 tons of bombs on the Fatherland. I wondered if they really didn't know they had lost the war.

My question was partially answered by a news flash on the BBC— Hitler had almost been assasinated! Apparently some of his high-ranking officers tried to blow the little bastard to Kingdom Come, and almost succeeded. This was the sole topic of conversation in the combat mess, and everybody had a smile on his face. This news probably wasn't as significant as the breakout at Saint Lô, but it boosted our morale.

The Group didn't fly for the next two days. Meanwhile I was given my Air Medal, along with forty or fifty other guys. The ceremony was impressive. Everybody wore Class-A uniforms, and we were divided into groups, some to receive the Air Medal, some the D.F.C. I was a little envious of the guys in the D.F.C. group; they were finished, or almost finished, with their tour. But I was very happy to get the little blue leatherette-covered case the C.O. handed me. After he shook hands, said "Congratulations" and moved on to the next man, I opened the case and looked at the medal. It was very impressive, an eagle with a lightning bolt in each talon. The medal hung on a blue and orange ribbon, and inserted in the velvet lining of the case was a miniature of the ribbon, done in porcelain enamel. It had a stud on the back, and was intended for wearing in the buttonhole of a civilian coat lapel. Wearing a civilian suit seemed a long way off.

Most of the awards were given for "successful completion of missions," but one bombardier from the 326th got a D.F.C. for a mission he led back in mid-June. Just before bombs-away, a flak burst hit the nose compartment and knocked him off the bombsight. The navigator was wounded as well. The bombardier just got back on the sight, made his last-minute corrections, and dropped squarely on the target. His D.F.C. was for "courage, coolness, and skill under fire." If he made it to the end of his tour, I thought, he would get an Oak Leaf Cluster to add to his D.F.C. ribbon.

After the awards ceremony ended, it dawned on me that I would soon be receiving an Oak Leaf Cluster to my Air Medal. Things were looking up. I had flown six missions in eleven days, and at that rate, by the end of July I'd be halfway through.

But that was not the way it worked out. By the end of July I was beginning to think they had misplaced my name and didn't know I was still available. The Group flew four missions during the last eight days of July, and I wasn't on the list for any of them. I realized that this was just the luck of the draw, but it made no sense to me to fly for three days in a row, then not be alerted for the next eight days. The four missions I missed were a mixed-bag—two tactical raids to France, two deep penetrations to Germany. The tactical raids were not too successful.

The July 24 mission called for strikes on targets in the Perrier–Saint Lô area. The weather was still uncooperative, and the battle lines on the ground were constantly changing. As a result, most of the groups were recalled without bombing. Some groups tried to find a target of opportunity but couldn't. An accidental release by one group, I didn't know which one, killed twenty U.S. soldiers and wounded sixty or seventy others. I'm certain it wasn't the Ninety-second. The guys I talked to said they hit the Primary target, with fairly good visibility in the area.

The mission on the twenty-fifth was a repeat performance, with even worse consequences. A couple of groups dropped short of the bomb line, and this time over a hundred U.S. troops were killed and almost four hundred wounded. I couldn't find out whether the Ninety-second was involved in these miscues or not. In fact, I wasn't sure whether anybody knew exactly what happened, or which groups were involved. The use of high-altitude strategic bombers for close support was a tricky proposition. We could bomb a factory with surgical precision from 28,000 feet; that's what the plane was designed to do, and what we were trained to do. Bombing from lower altitudes, in close proximity to a fluid battle line, and in marginal weather, was very risky indeed. Despite the extreme care taken to locate our own troops' positions, and our being cautioned that we should not release if there was any doubt, there was a good chance that some mistakes would be made. The mistakes made on July 24 and 25 resulted in tragic consequences.

After a two-day stand-down, the Group went out again on the twenty-eighth, this time to Merseburg. I was just as glad not to be on this one. Another two-day stand-down on the twenty-ninth and thirtieth, and I asked the squadron exec for a pass to London. He hedged a little, and said he'd let me know.

Late in July, General Hap Arnold sent a message to the Eighth Air Force. I suppose it was intended to boost morale. The message began by saying, "The continued all-out efforts by your heavies day after day is most gratifying." My morale was OK, but it was better when I was flying, instead of just sitting around day after day, waiting to see my name on the Alert List or to get an OK on my request for a pass to London. I'd rather have the pass, but eventually I had to get back in the air.

On the last day of July I got a three-day pass, to begin August 2. The Group had gone to Munich on the day I found out about my pass being OK'd, and between missing the mission and getting the pass, I felt twice-blessed.

It would be nice to get away for a few days and I was delighted at the prospect of spending three days in London. The train was packed, but I found a seat in a car that wasn't divided into compartments like the one I had taken on the first trip. It had a narrow aisle down the center with seats or either side.

At Luton more passengers got on and I got up to give my seat to a woman. I walked to the back of the car and stood on the little platform at the end, between the cars, where I spent the rest of the trip talking with a British corporal about his experiences and mine—mostly about his. He had been at Dunkirk early in the war, and now was just back from North Africa. He was a friendly fellow, with a heavy accent which I thought was Scottish, but he said he was from the north of England. He was very grateful for my American cigarettes, and smoked three or four during the hour or so from Luton to London. As we pulled into St. Pancras, I made him take a few more cigarettes, which he put in his pocket very carefully. I would have given him the rest of the pack, but it was more than half full, and I hadn't had a carton from my folks in a while. I had two packs in my musette bag, which meant that I would probably wind up smoking Player's Weights before I left London.

I took a taxi from St. Pancras to the Regent Palace Hotel, and had absolutely no luck at all. They were booked up solid. The desk clerk recommended a couple of others I might try—the Strand Palace, the Aldwych. They were full, too. I was getting discouraged. I didn't want to stay at the Red Cross Club. From what I'd heard it was too much like a barracks. I finally got into a taxi and threw myself on the mercy of the driver. He suggested a hotel he knew of in Russell Square, and I agreed that would be fine. I was desperate.

It turned out that Russell Square was almost back at St. Pancras. And the hotel didn't resemble a hotel at all, just a doorway among a bunch of doorways in a block-long building. The lobby looked more like a large living room, with sofas and chairs and end tables. But it was pleasant; not posh, but pleasant. I got a room on the ground floor, just to the left of the reception desk. It was tiny and the bath was down the hall. But I was only going to sleep here.

I had a marvellous time exploring the great city on my own, going wherever I pleased, whenever I pleased. I toured several of the museums, and strolled through Green Park, and Hyde Park, and St.

James's Park. I walked down streets without knowing their names, looking at old buildings decorated with lions and gargoyles. I seldom passed a pub without going in for a mild-and-bitter—unless the pub was closed. Often they were. I hadn't yet learned the opening and closing times; most seemed to close at two in the afternoon and reopen about four, yet some were open all afternoon.

I walked the Thames embankment, occasionally venturing down a stone staircase to the water's edge and gazing down the river from a damp, moss-covered boat landing. I was fascinated by the fat gray barrage balloons wallowing in the air above the river, tethered by steel cables. These ungainly gas-filled sausages could be seen everywhere around the city. I remembered a cartoon in *Yank* magazine that pictured two American G.I.'s walking in London gazing up at half a dozen barrage balloons, on a dreary, rainy day. One of them was saying to the other, "I wonder why they don't just cut the cables and let the damn place sink!"

I even looked up 221B Baker Street. It was an office of some sort, and it didn't look like Sherlock Holmes's residence at all. I walked on up Baker Street and found myself at Madame Tussaud's Wax Museum. I bought a ticket and went inside, and was immediately embarassed when I tried for a moment or two to give my ticket to a uniformed attendant with an outstretched hand. It turned out to be a wax figure. I had never seen wax figures before, and these were incredibly lifelike. The Nazi group was particularly interesting—Hitler, Goering, Goebbels, and the rest. And I was amused to see that Rudolf Hess was separated from the others, standing alone in a glass enclosure! The British sense of humor was not impaired by war.

I spent three very enjoyable hours in the museum, and when I left I made a mental note to come back again. I wanted to spend more time in the Chamber of Horrors. The grisly scenes of axe-murders, executions by hanging, guillotine, and other interesting methods, and the special section devoted to Jack the Ripper deserved a second look. Sometime when I'm in London and had nothing better to do, I promised myself, I would spend a couple of hours in that macabre chamber, preferably with a date.

I took in London from one end to the other, soaking up the sights and sounds and the feeling of the city. The buzz bombs were continuing to menace the city, more so than when I was in town a month ago. The weird chattering sound of the flying bombs, the eerie silence after the sound stopped, and then the earth-shaking explosion twenty seconds later became part of the daily routine—and the nightly routine as well.

London after dark, blacked out but not totally dark in the pale summer moonlight, displayed a spectral beauty that I had not seen on the first visit. Trafalgar Square in the moonlight was particularly beautiful. Across the square I could make out the ornate columns of the National Gallery, faintly illuminated by the moonlight. A taxi crept slowly past the lions of the Nelson monument, following a slow-moving, ghostly little puddle of light made by the slit in its single headlight.

I was in love with London, and it was as if I had it all to myself. I had been looking forward for a month to coming back, and had wondered if the reality of the visit would be as good as the anticipation. And there had been a question in my mind about whether I might have had a better time if I'd come with some of my friends. No, absolutely not. During these three days in London I got to know the city, and love it, in a very personal way. I don't think I would have had the same feeling with a bunch of friends arguing about where to go and what to do next.

And I wasn't alone the whole time. I shared most of the second day, and part of the night, with a good-looking W.A.A.F. sergeant named Kay. Our meeting was very straightforward and not at all accidental. She was window-shopping along Shaftesbury and I just joined her. I didn't give her a line, but just said, "Hi—mind if I walk along with you?" She smiled and said, "Not at all," and that was that.

She was tall and sort of willowy, very pretty and outgoing. She had been in the RAF since 1941, and I guessed that she was about twenty-four or twenty-five. She was stationed at RAF Stoke-Heath in Shropshire.

"Where is Shropshire—near London?"

"No, afraid not. It's in the northwest country. A bit beyond Birmingham."

"What sort of airbase is it? Bombers?"

"Training, actually. It's called an O.T.U. Let me give you my address."

Kay was in London for the same reason I was, to get away from the base for awhile and have a good time. We hit it off very well, and spent the afternoon sightseeing and talking. Although she was not more familiar with London than I was, when I brought up the subject of dinner she did know a few places. We wound up in a semi-fancy restaurant and spent a couple of hours at the bar before we had dinner. She liked gin-and-orange; four or five of them didn't faze her at all. She loved to talk and we covered just about every subject, but mostly we talked about flying and the war. She wanted to know how many "ops" I'd done, and I had to request clarification.

"Ops. You know, flight operations."

"Oh, you mean missions. I've flown an even dozen."

I didn't try to impress Kay about my exploits as a combat flyer. She'd been in the RAF almost since the Battle of Britain, and I knew she'd been around combat flyers for years—dashing Spitfire pilots like I'd seen in the war movies, no doubt. But she was impressed by our doctrine of daylight bombing. She asked about this several times, almost as if she didn't quite believe that we'd be so foolish as to venture into Germany in daylight in a slow-flying bomber. I knew that the RAF had tried this earlier and had suffered such heavy losses that they decided to switch over to bombing at night. They called it "carpet bombing," which I thought was another way of saying they didn't expect accuracy, just overall saturation of a city.

After dinner we found ourselves walking along Piccadilly. It was as if everybody was drawn to that place, particularly at night. It seemed to be the only place in London that was as filled with as many people at night as during the daytime. Kay was staying with a family in London. My efforts to lure her to my hotel in Russell Square were unsuccessful, and after she insisted that she must call it a night I walked her to their flat. I have no idea where it was, and she had some difficulty finding it, but after about twenty minutes she said this was it and I walked part-way up a darkened stairway with her. We sat on the stairs for awhile saying goodnight, and this turned into a sort of wrestling match, which she won. After I promised I'd write, I left and started looking for a taxi. I wondered whether I'd given up too easily; she was definitely in a romantic mood.

From what I gathered when we discussed the English people, my reaction was different from many of the Americans in England. I really liked them, and sort of adapted to their ways, such as tea in the afternoon, and speaking precise English. None of my friends accused me of getting an English accent, but I was more and more using words and phrases that I picked up from my encounters with English men and women.

It's possible that a lot of American G.I.'s mistook the English trait of acting and speaking with precision for coolness and aloofness. For example, many times in London I'd ask an Englishman how to get to a particular place. Invariably the answer would be phrased like this:

"Righto," while he thought for a few seconds. Then, "Keep on along here," he would generally point up or down the street, "second right, first left, carry on about a hundred yards . . . you *cawn't* miss it."

If I asked for directions in Dallas, the answer would be more like this: "Lessee, keep on this street 'til you come to Elm, then make a right and keep going 'til you hit Ervay. Turn left on there and I think it's about the middle of the block!"

The English way might not have sounded as friendly as the American, but it really was. It was just much more precise, and actually less confusing. However, the part about "you cawn't miss it" was not necessarily true. I did, many times. But it was not the fault of the instructions; it was only that London was an eleventh-century city laid out in a higgledy-piggledy fashion and the "second right" would turn out to be what I thought was a narrow little entrance to a private home, when in actuality it was a street.

That three-day pass to London was everything I expected it to be. And more. I relived it in my mind on the train ride back to Wellingborough, and already I was thinking about the things I wanted to do *next* trip. I wanted to find a hotel somewhere in Soho. Russell Square was just too far from the action and the neighborhood was just a little depressing. If I had any advance notice I could write for reservations at the Regent Palace, but I couldn't expect to get an OK on a pass more than a day in advance.

Combat flying was a strange way to fight a war. Here I had been in London for three glorious days, enjoying the restaurants, and the shops, and the pubs, and the girls. Nobody was shooting at me, and except for the remote possibility of being under a buzz bomb when it exploded, I might have been spending a fun weekend in Dallas. And for ten days before that I had lazed around the base just trying to find something to occupy my time. I hadn't been inside a B-17 for two weeks. Yet two weeks ago I had flown five missions in six days. I had been tired, and tense, with my guts knotted up when I saw B-17s like ours blow up over a place I had just bombed or was about to bomb. And tomorrow or the next day I could be back over Germany again.

For now, however, the reality was still London—walking aimlessly, and marvelling at the ethereal beauty of the city at night, and the uncanny realism of the wax figures at Tussaud's. Munich and Peenemünde and Köthen and the other places seemed like a long-ago dream.

I got off the train at Wellingborough and walked through the little station to the parking lot where the Liberty Run trucks were parked. I was looking forward to telling the guys in the hut all about my experiences in London. Moore would want to know all the details, especially about the little W.A.A.F. sergeant. Maybe I would tell him I scored with her; he'd be disappointed if I didn't. A truck driver finally walked up and asked, "Anybody for the Podington Express?"

I walked into the hut, swinging my musette bag and smiling, ready to announce my return from the big city. But nobody was there. There were no lights on, and it took me a few seconds before I noticed the rolled-up mattresses on the bunks. I was standing in front of what used to be Hanley's bunk, but there were no clothes on the rack, no sheets or blankets on the bed. Just the mattress, rolled back so that the springs showed up against the floor. Horton's, Brewer's, and Moore's were the same—everything gone except the mattresses.

I knew in an instant what had happened. I just didn't know how, or when, or where. I turned on the light and walked down to my bunk and dropped the musette bag on it. The other two guys still lived here; their bunks were made up and their clothes were still hanging on the racks. They'd know what happened, but they weren't around.

I walked to the hut next door and went inside. Two guys were stretched out on their bunks, and one was sitting at the table reading. I knew them only fairly well. They knew who I was. One of them asked, "Just get back from London?"

"Yeah, just now. What the hell happened to my buddies?"

"They got it yesterday over Merk-something-or-other."

"Merseburg?"

"No, but it sounds something like it. Just barely in Germany, close to the French border."

"What was it, flak?"

"Fighters. They shot hell out of the Group. We lost two planes over the target, and another one crash-landed here."

"Did you see what happened? Did anybody bail out?"

"We weren't on the mission, but somebody told me there were several parachutes, so I'm sure some of them got out."

I walked over to the squadron office to try to get more details, but really didn't learn much, except that I was alerted to fly tomorrow.

It took a couple of days to piece together what had happened. The target was an oil refinery at Merkwiller, not far from Strasbourg. After bombs-away the Group made a wide turn—a couple of guys said they were making a three-sixty, although I can't understand why that would have been necessary. The German fighters jumped them while they were in the turn. They shot down two planes and damaged most of the others. There were several parachutes seen; just how many depended on who I was talking to. Nobody had time to watch any particular plane. They were too busy trying to defend themselves. The fighter attack was sudden and savage. And my old crew was gone, either dead or somewhere in Germany.

Before I hit the sack that night I was going through my B-4 bag looking for something and there was Hanley's Colt .45 pistol. Just before my pass to London, he'd asked me if I'd strip it down and clean it for him. He knew I was familiar with guns and apparently he didn't even know how to field-strip a forty-five. I don't think he ever carried it on missions. It was still full of Cosmoline grease, and it didn't look like the clip had ever been loaded.

He was probably just as well off not having it when he bailed out. If he bailed out. I made a mental note to take it over to Ordnance and turn it in. Then I hit the sack and lay there for several hours thinking about the twist of fate that had intervened when I was given the option to change my MOS (Military Occupation Specialty) and become a bombardier back in June. If I hadn't changed crews, I would have been over Merkwiller yesterday. I tried to get to sleep. I had to fly tomorrow.

The loss of my old crew mates bothered me more than my matter-of-fact conversations would indicate. Losses were a regular part of combat flying, and we talked about them in the same dispassionate way that we talked about routine things. But I *knew* these guys. I tried to picture what it was like for them in those few terrifying minutes. Somebody said the tail guns and the ball turret never even moved after the German fighters started firing, and that didn't sound like Moore and Horton survived. Somebody else said he thought the waist gunner was blown right out of the midsection. That would be Brewer, the easy-going, taciturn farm boy. Maybe he was able to pull his parachute handle. I tried to figure how the guys up front made out, but apparently the airplane broke in half just back of the radio room, and the forward part must have plunged straight down.

I didn't feel guilty about thanking God I wasn't with them. I might well find myself in the same situation tomorrow. Yet for some reason, I didn't think so. It happened to other guys, not to me. That was probably what they had thought, too.

TEN

AIR OFFENSIVE: RHINELAND

The morning after I got back from London it was business as usual. We crossed the Dutch coast, and I spotted the familiar islands stretching north from the entrance to the Zuider Zee. Some of them I could name without even referring to the map. We were headed for Hannover, in north-central Germany, to drop some bombs on Langenhagen Airfield. I wondered if the Messerschmitts would venture out today.

Actually, I had had a nagging curiosity about enemy fighters for some time, and kind of wanted to see one. But I decided I didn't want to see one today; maybe later. And maybe not at all would be better still, after what they had done to my old crew. Maybe fighters *were* more dangerous than flak. They had shot down two of our B-17s—three if you counted the one that crash-landed and burned on the runway—and made a lot of holes in the rest of our airplanes. I wonder how many fighters there were over Merkwiller? Nobody I had talked with was certain.

We didn't see any Messerschmitts over Langenhagen and didn't lose any of our Forts. There was plenty of flak, but it did more damage to our nerves than to our airplanes.

Coming back from Hannover I got the scare of my life. We were about an hour from the Dutch coast and I was leaning forward in the nose, watching other bomb groups and then peering at the landscape below us. I spotted a town just ahead of us and a little to the left, and started to reach back for the map to see if I could identify it. Before I could get the map, the ground started to light up with small flashes. First a dozen, then a hundred little flashes of fire in and around the town, until the whole area was covered with what I automatically assumed were flashes from antiaircraft batteries. I think my heart stopped, momentarily. I just sat there frozen with dread, expecting any second to see the black puffs of flak from what must be two or three hundred flak guns.

I recovered enough to push the intercom button, and was about to scream a warning when I spotted a group of B-24s over that sea of flashes. And they weren't getting any flak, not a burst. They were about 5,000 feet below us, just crossing over the town. I realized that I was seeing their bomb bursts on the ground. I already had the intercom open, so I said, as calmly as I could at the moment, "Look down at ten o'clock. Some B-24s are tearing up a town."

"Yeah, I see them. Looks like they dropped incendiaries."

I decided not to tell anybody about my near heart attack, and called for an oxygen check. I wondered whether I was getting flak-happy.

I flew the next day, and the day after that, then skipped a day and flew another one. The weather was perfect, and the Eighth was taking advantage of it, after the unexpected and unpredictable fronts that had plagued us for the past two weeks, either keeping us on the ground or else making us fly around trying to find a target we could see. Eight missions had been scrubbed during July, six of them after briefing. But August was shaping up like it would be a banner month.

On the sixth we went to Brandenburg to bomb an aircraft assembly plant. This was another long haul, just a few miles from Berlin. We nailed the target beautifully, but again the Germans made us pay. The First Division had Brandenburg all to ourselves, with about 200 B-17s over the target. Eleven were shot down and 106 damaged, but the Ninety-second got off pretty easy. We didn't lose a plane, just brought back some holes and feathered engines. On the seventh we took out another bridge in France, at a place called Nanteuil. This was my fifteenth mission, and it was a genuine milk run.

The Group went back to France on the eighth but I wasn't alerted. I was glad to have some time to sack out. The three in a row I had just flown left me tired and in need of sleep. I doubted I'd had more than fifteen hours sleep in three days.

Briefing on August 9 was once again dominated by the weather officer, who talked about slow-moving fronts and the possibility of heavy cloud cover. We were going to southeast Germany today to hit some factories and oil refineries, but the weathermen didn't seem too optimistic about our chances of hitting the primary target.

They were right. The weather deteriorated so badly that most of the Second and Third Division groups were recalled. We bombed Karlsruhe, finally, and I think we hit the marshaling yards. We were lucky to find a target of opportunity and get credit for the mission. For most of the Eighth Air Force, today might as well have been a practice mission. But I got to log another one. The second page of my mission log was half filled.

I had new roommates, but I'd been flying almost every day and hadn't gotten to know much about them. They had been flying practice missions, getting ready to start their combat tour. The guy who took the bunk next to mine was a strange sort. He was very serious, almost sour, and he didn't talk much. He acted like combat flying wasn't new to him, never asked any questions about how bad the flak was, or even about what happened to the guys who used to live here. His name was Bob Danielson and he came from Wyoming.

The tail gunner on that crew was a short, sleepy-eyed fellow from New Jersey named Jack Fromkin. He and I became friends right away. He was outgoing and friendly, not at all looking forward to flying combat, and he didn't mind saying so. He had a droll sense of humor and seemed to be well educated.

One afternoon at the Aero Club I made the mistake of asking Jack if he'd like to play a couple of games of Ping-Pong. He said he wouldn't mind, but he hadn't played in awhile. I fancied myself as an above average player, and figured I had a pigeon. I didn't. He absolutely slaughtered me. He played in a relaxed, dreamy style, never seeming to move very fast, never showing any emotion. He just sent the ball across the net like a bullet, sometimes playing from six or eight feet behind the table. He'd let one of my best slams get almost to the floor, then just pick it up with his paddle and I wouldn't even see the ball when it hit my side of the table and whistled past me. In three games I don't think I got a total of six points!

Finally I said, "Hell, I give up. Let's get a beer." He grinned and laid his paddle down. We walked back to the bar and I asked, "How did you get so damn good at the game?"

"Played a lot before I went in the Air Corps. Actually, I was New Jersey State Champion."

"The hell you were!"

"I really was. And I was tennis champion for about twenty minutes." He explained that the other guy didn't show up for the match, and they awarded it to him on default. Then, when the other guy did arrive, Jack agreed to play him. That turned out to be a mistake, because he got whipped in straight sets.

After two days of inactivity, with the Group on stand-down, I was rested and ready to go on the twelfth. We dumped a few tons of bombs on a German fighter park in France, at a place called Chaumont, and got home early. We encountered only a little token flak, and I was delighted to chalk up two milk runs in a row. And at briefing the next day, it looked like another one. We were going to France again, a little town called Evreux. It was only a few miles inland, just south of Rouen, and not much farther than my first little trip across the Channel to Calais.

But Evreux didn't turn out the way I expected. The Germans had a couple of flak batteries that were manned by experts. The deputy lead plane, flying right alongside us, took a direct hit between the fuselage and number three engine. The Fort flipped over and hung upside down for a long while, burning fiercely, before it finally slid away toward the green patchwork of the French countryside.

It was the most shocking thing that I'd seen. Being so close was part of it, and knowing that my friend Tom Crosby was in the nose made it very personal. But the horror of it was the fact that the airplane was upside down. And it hung there, in that unnatural position, for such a long time—or what seemed like a long time. I couldn't get that terrible picture out of my mind.

We lost only the one Fort over Evreux, and saw hardly more than a half-dozen flak bursts, but almost every plane in the Group took a few hits. A couple had engines shot out and feathered props. I wondered how a few flak guns could do that much damage. I decided that maybe there was no such thing as a milk run. Or maybe *every* mission was a milk run . . . if you survived it. One thing seemed certain: if you kept flying over Europe and getting shot at every time, it was just a matter of time before you would get hit! One burst of flak, in the right place, was all it took to make a B-17 a statistic.

Evreux was my eighteenth mission. I was now over the hump, more than halfway through with my tour. When I logged the mission in my little book, I made a cryptic notation about Crosby. I really didn't need to. I wouldn't forget it.

The Group went to Germany on August 14, but I didn't go. They bombed somewhere around Luxembourg, and didn't lose any airplanes. I was alerted for the next day, and wondered whether we'd go to Germany or France. Somehow, after yesterday, it didn't seem to make a lot of difference. We went back to Germany, as it turned out, and bombed another Luftwaffe base. This one was at Eschborn, just outside Frankfurt. I was apprehensive, more so than usual. As we got closer to Frankfurt I was very tense, watching the other planes in the squadron and hoping none of them turned into a fireball right before my eyes. When the pilot's voice suddenly announced that we were coming up on the I.P., I was startled.

As we headed for the target there was the usual canopy of flak over the city, but no fighters were coming at us and none of our B-17s were being turned into blazing, airborne wreckage, although there were some close bursts. Then, just into the bomb run, when I had my eyes fixed steadily on the lead plane, I saw it take what I first thought was a direct hit. The Fort seemed to stagger for a split second, then straightened out and we dropped without any further incident.

Now it was our turn. The instant I hit the bomb switch our B-17 lurched upward like a rearing horse. I could feel the pilot fighting the airplane to get the nose back down, but we hadn't been hit, as far as I could tell. It dawned on me, finally, that we were carrying four one-ton bombs today, and I had dropped "salvo;" they all went together. Most of the time we had carried more bombs and less weight. The normal load, if there was any such thing as that, was twelve 500-pounders. I always expected the plane to buck upwards when the bombs were salvoed, but not like today's violent surge. The additional weight was part of the reason, plus the fact that four bombs left the plane at virtually the same instant.

It was the next day that we learned what had happened to the lead plane. The flak burst exploded just under the nose of the lead ship and the bombardier, a Chinese-American named William Chun was hit in the leg by several pieces of jagged shrapnel. He got back on the bombsight and didn't say a word until after bombs-away. We nailed the target, putting almost every bomb within a few yards of the M.P.I. Chun's injuries weren't fatal, but they were apparently very, very painful. He was recommended for a D.F.C. for courage and coolness under fire. He certainly deserved it.

Chun's experience made me wonder how I'd react if I got hit. I guess nobody could predict what he would do until it actually happened. I fervently hoped it wouldn't happen.

After Frankfurt they seemed to forget about me again. After two missions that I wasn't alerted for, with a stand-down in between, I put in for another pass. I really didn't expect it to go through, but it did. I signed out Monday morning, August 20, and for the third time took the little train we called the "Toonerville Trolley." I watched the increasingly familiar fields and stone fences of the Midlands roll past my window and felt serene. It seemed strange, but I wasn't worried about the future, just looking forward to London. It occurred to me that I was more than halfway through my tour and nobody had said anything about me going to the "flak house" yet. That was routine; at about the midpoint of a tour, you were detached for two weeks' rest and rehabilitation at a manor house somewhere. This was supposed to let your nerves calm down, just sitting around and taking walks in the country. Some of the guys who had been to R&R said it was okay, but it got boring after a while.

I wondered why nobody had mentioned to me that I should go. I really didn't feel I needed any R&R; my nerves were fine, and I didn't have any real symptoms of being flak-happy. Maybe it would come up when I got back. Perhaps I could pass up the flak house in exchange for a two-day pass to London every two weeks.

I grabbed a taxi at St. Pancras and when the driver asked where to, I just said, "Piccadilly." He was a grizzled old guy, squarejawed and brusque. I asked him about hotels in the central area of Soho, and at first he was pretty noncommittal. I kept talking to him, badgering him, but in a friendly way, and by the time we got to Charing Cross Road, he admitted somewhat grudgingly that he did know a nice little hotel right near Piccadilly, that usually had some rooms. It was a bit off the beaten track, he said, at a place where most people wouldn't expect to find a hotel. I thanked him for the information and said let's give it a try.

The taxi turned off Piccadilly toward St. James's Park, then turned again onto a little narrow street running parallel to Piccadilly. I asked the driver what street this was.

"Jermyn Street . . . the 'otel's called the Winston . . . there it is on the left."

The front doors to the Winston were set back under a marquee that looked as if it belonged to a theatre. I walked into the lobby and looked around. It was small, and had a pleasant feeling about it. The reception counter was on the left, and there were half a dozen people, all of them in uniform, talking to a couple of clerks. Since there wasn't a queue all the way out to the sidewalk, I decided there was no big hurry, and I could size up the place before I committed myself. I walked over to a desk at the opposite end of the lobby that had a sign on it saying, "Head Porter." Sitting behind the desk was a man dressed in a black coat with silk lapels, and the left lapel had a row of miniature medals pinned to it. He was in his fifties, I judged, and had a withered left hand. He smiled and nodded, and I offered him a Lucky Strike.

Half an hour and several cigarettes later, the old fellow had told me all about his experiences in World War I when he was in the Royal something-or-other Fusiliers. George had also filled me in on the blitz, the night of the Great Fire in London, and miscellaneous other bits of information. I wasn't just listening to kill time; I was interested, and I guess he could tell it. He commented on my Air Medal and Oak Leaf Cluster and asked how many operations I'd flown.

I wasn't sure exactly what his job was. Finally I suggested that I'd better go see about getting a room. I asked my new friend the head porter if the rooms were okay. He said they were very nice. "Not the Ritz, mind you, but quite comfortable—and the restaurant puts up a very good meal."

I told him I'd enjoyed chatting with him, and took out a fresh pack of Luckies and handed it to him. He seemed overwhelmed by my generosity, and when he finished thanking me, suggested, "Look 'ere, Yank, why don't you just leave your bag with me and go 'ave lunch. I'll see to your room."

I walked around the corner to Piccadilly and wound up drinking my lunch at the American Bar. After several Scotches and an interesting chat with an RAF sergeant pilot, two RCAF air crewmen and a British officer who wore a maroon beret, I started wondering about my room. And my musette bag. The more I wondered the more I worried, so I took my leave and walked back to the Winston.

My friend at the desk stood up when I walked over and handed me my musette bag and my room key. I thanked him for his kindness and then, for no reason that I could explain, opened my bag and handed him an almost full carton of Luckies. I don't know whether I'd had too much to drink, or was just relieved that he had done what he said he would. But the result was that I seemed to have made a friend for life. Anytime I was in London, just drop in, he said. Never mind the receptions desk; and he'd take care of me.

By the time I got settled in my room and washed up it was almost three o'clock, and I hadn't had any lunch yet. I took the lift down to the first floor restaurant to have a bite. It was called l'Auberge de France, and it looked very posh to me. In fact, the hotel was much nicer inside than I had expected, judging from the outside appearance. I picked a table at a window overlooking Jermyn Street. The table was next to a grand piano, so I assumed someone played during the dinner hour.

The waitress was decked out in a frilly apron and cap, like the movie version of a French maid. She was tall, well built, red-haired, and had a rich Irish brogue. She smiled and asked if I'd like tea.

"Actually I'd like a bite to eat, maybe a sandwich or something."

She explained that "tea" was a light meal, and I was just in time for high tea. So I had my first real introduction into the English custom of afternoon tea. I almost emptied a tray of watercress and cucumber sandwiches and finished up with sweets, tarts, scones, and other things I'd heard about but not tried. It was more relaxed than a meal, and I divided my time between flirting with the Irish waitress and eyeing a good looking W.A.A.F. sitting alone at a table in the center of the restaurant. She was having tea too and since she was alone I decided I'd see if I could change that. I asked the waitress where the men's room was located, and got up from the table. I walked past the W.A.A.F. and gave her a good looking over. Her tunic was unbuttoned, and as I passed I saw her tie clip. It was a U.S. colonel's eagle! She smiled, but I realized I was outranked and decided to concentrate on the waitress.

The colonel showed up before I left, but by that time I had convinced the Irish waitress to go out with me that night and show me a bit of London after dark. She had the impression that this was my first trip to the city and I decided to let her go on thinking that. I played the part of the young American airman who wanted to see the big city and didn't know where to start. When I found out her name was Kay, I wondered if there was something about that name that attracted me to a girl.

This Kay was quite different than the little W.A.A.F. of the same name. She liked to dance and drink. She drank beer, and could handle her pints of bitter as well as I could, if not better. But she was a bit on the serious side; perhaps "intense" was a better word. We wound up in a big, boisterous night club called the Universelle Brasserie. I would never have found it by myself. It was just a doorway in the Criterion Building near Piccadilly Circus. A stairway led down to the lower level. The place had two or three bars and was filled with noise, smoke, and people sitting around little tables no bigger than dinner plates. As we worked our way through the mass of humanity, I saw every conceivable kind of uniform, including many I couldn't possibly identify. There were some civilians, but they were greatly outnumbered by the military. And there seemed to be plenty of girls to go around.

Kay spotted a table and grabbed it while I went to get a couple of pints. We drank bitter and talked and watched people come and go for a couple of hours. I was having a great time, and so was everybody else. The place was a madhouse.

After we left the Brasserie I walked Kay to her bus stop, and we made light conversation as we made our way along the dark little streets. "Kay, how come you're not back in Ireland, away from the war?"

"Oh, I chose to spend the war in London."

"Why?"

"Partly for the pleasure of seeing the English get bombed."

She said this matter-of-factly, not in anger, but not as if she were kidding, either. I said, "Come on, Kay, you shouldn't joke about that."

She responded with a little smile. "I'm not joking."

"You don't mean you want England to lose the war!"

"Not really, no—but London *is* the capital and should be bombed in any case. And if I happen to enjoy it, it's my own business."

It was hard for me to believe she really meant what she was saying. I knew that there were problems between the Irish and the English, but I had no idea the feeling could go that far. Kay didn't seem to have any bitterness toward the English, at least none that showed. She didn't tell jokes about them, or make snide remarks. I never was certain whether she really felt the way she said she did. Anyway, she was a girl, and a good-looking one, and she seemed to like me. So I decided to forget about politics and just enjoy her company.

I stopped in l'Auberge the next afternoon and had a cup of tea and a chat with Kay. She asked if I planned to stay here next time I came to London, and when I said I did she smiled and said, "Good. See you then, I hope." She couldn't spend much time chatting, she said, because the lady in charge of the restaurant was hovering nearby.

I took a late train back to Wellingborough on Tuesday, and it was dark before I got there. Earlier I had had half a mind to stay a few hours longer and take the *last* train. I wanted to walk the streets of London in the moonlight. But I wasn't sure there would be a moon tonight, and I might screw up and miss the last train. I never liked to cut things so close. The thought of being alerted for a mission and not showing up scared me. They'd probably court-martial me.

For some reason I wasn't worried about the sixteen missions I still had left to fly. The only thing I was concerned about at the moment was how soon I could slip through another two-day pass to London.

I signed in and checked the bulletin board and there was no Alert List posted. I turned and asked the duty sergeant if the Group had flown yesterday or today. He said, "Nope, still on stand-down." The only thing of interest on the bulletin board was a notice that Glenn Miller, now *Major* Glenn Miller, and his orchestra would give a concert at the Ninety-second on the twenty-third. I took that to mean we would probably be on stand-down until the twenty-fourth.

There was a blackjack game in full swing when I walked into the hut. Jack Fromkin yelled, "Hey, Koger, get over here, we need some new blood in the game!" I assumed he was winning. I hung my coat on the rack, took off my tie and got into the game. A master sergeant from the medical detachment had brought a couple of fifths of "after mission" whisky, and everybody was getting loaded—everybody except my new next bunk neighbor Danielson. He wasn't drinking, nor was he laughing or talking. He was just playing cards, wearing that serious expression. Occasionally he'd get irritated when the game was delayed while we all poured a glass of Scotch, and say, "Come on, dammit, let's get on with the game!" That was about the limit of his conversation. I couldn't figure Danielson out. He seemed to be mad at the world in general, and I wondered why.

On Wednesday Glenn Miller's band played to a packed house. In addition to every man in the Group, we had a thousand or so come over from Chelveston and Thurleigh, the other two groups in our Wing. I had thought they might bring in some girls from the local towns, and I did finally spot a few, but they were scattered among more than two thousand men and I never got close to one.

I was still humming "Moonlight Serenade" when I checked the Alert List. A maximum effort scheduled for tomorrow. Life was not just partying in London and listening to Glenn Miller. I was going back to work for a living.

ELEVEN

A PLACE CALLED MERSEBURG

There really was no need to look for checkpoints on the patch-work of the earth below or to try to identify rivers or towns that would pinpoint our position. But this is what I was doing, glancing from the map to the ground below, wasting my time just like I had wasted it that morning at bombardiers' briefing studying the maps and aerial photographs. For the last half hour I had known where our target was. It was directly under that ugly, out-of-place black cloud that hung in the pale blue August sky off to the right.

I had been watching that incongruous blot in the sky for some time, trying to convince myself that maybe it wasn't our target. We weren't turning toward it, not yet anyway. We flew straight on and I thought that perhaps, for reasons unknown to me, we were going to bypass it and go bomb a target of opportunity somewhere.

Nonsense. At briefing this morning the G-2 officer had talked for a long time about Merseburg, the number one target on the Priority List. And he added that it was now the most heavily defended target in Germany, with more flak guns than Berlin itself. To underscore the comments from G-2, a guy in the equipment room was talking about his trip to Merseburg back in May. As he struggled into his heated suit, he said, "They got more damn flak guns than Carter's got liver pills!" From where I sat right now I would have to agree. I watched the ominous black cloud and figured it would be about twenty minutes before we made our turn to the right and headed into it, to replace those 400 poor bastards who were in there right at this moment. From this distance, the B-17s weren't visible, but I knew they were right in the middle of that storm of flak. That was the reason for the cloud in the first place—because they were there. But in just a few minutes they'd be out of it, maybe minus a few planes, and it would be our turn. I had never before felt such a terrible dread.

By the time we started our bomb run the black cloud would be a faded, washed-out gray, and the individual puffs would be shapeless gray smudges, dissipating in the winds aloft. But they would begin again when we arrived, and the new puffs wouldn't be shapeless. They would be well-defined, like an hourglass standing upright, and they would be coal black. When we flew out of it—*if* we flew out of it—maybe I could watch the group following us as they went in and triggered the same phenomenon.

I called for an oxygen check and wondered why we hadn't turned. While the guys were reporting back with their OKs we started a slow turn to the right. Without even thinking about it I instinctively reached up and pulled my flying goggles down over the oxygen mask. The lead plane's bomb bay doors were coming open and I was calm and detached as I flipped my switches and set up the Intervalometer. My voice sounded almost bored over the intercom. "Doors open."

"Fighters. Nine o'clock level." I don't know which gunner called the warning. It really wasn't a warning so much as a notification. I glanced to the left and made out four planes in the distance. They were probably a mile away, much too far to identify, and flying parallel to our course.

"I think they're P-51s," somebody said. I agreed silently. Our escort fighters always flew in echelons of four. Promptly I forgot about the fighters and gave the bombardier's panel a last check to be sure everything was turned on.

It was about two minutes later that I took my eyes off the lead plane's belly to have a look at the target that was coming up ahead of us. Before my eyes focused on the ground, I caught a glimpse of four fighters—the same four I had just seen off to our left, I assumed. They were sweeping across in front of our formation in a wide one-eighty, coming around behind us. The lead fighter was closer than the other three and I concentrated my gaze on him. I couldn't make out exactly what type it was, but it looked to me like the wings were swept back almost to the rear end of the fuselage. And unless my eyes were deceiving me, it didn't have a horizontal stabilizer. And it was moving fast, really fast. Sure as hell it was no P-51! I decided I'd better sound some sort of an alarm, but calmly—

"Fighters coming around. One o'clock low—now two o'clock. Can you see them?"

"Yeah, I see them. What the hell *are* they?" That was the copilot's voice.

The pilot warned the gunners to keep a sharp eye and stay off the intercom unless it was absolutely necessary.

By now the fighters were out of my sight, headed back toward our rear, and I went back to watching the belly of the lead plane. I made a valiant effort to ignore the flak and just concentrate on the lead plane's bomb bay, but it was impossible. The flak was everywhere. And suddenly, mixed in with the big bursts I saw miniature bursts of flak. I wondered what the hell was going on; I'd never seen *small* flak! No more than two seconds after the smaller bursts started the tail gunner's voice burst through my headphones: "Fighters attacking, six o'clock!"

The shrill, excited voice was still ringing in my ears when a little gray shape flashed directly under our plane. I caught a momentary glimpse of a fat, bullet-shaped plane with wings swept back toward the tail in a V. It had no tail that I could see, but it did have a black cross on the wing. The little fighter trailed a white streamer like a contrail, and in an instant it was a thousand yards ahead of us. I saw a puff of black smoke from its tail, then another, as it pulled up and climbed almost vertically. I stared at it incredulously as it continued to climb—straight up! It was probably 5,000 feet above us when I lost sight of it.

I looked back at the lead plane and at the same time swung the chin turret control column to the ready position in front of me. I flipped the gun switches up to firing position, still trying to keep my eyes on the lead plane. It seemed like all hell was breaking loose. The flak was the worst I'd ever seen. I could hear it as it smashed against the plane, and I knew it was tearing holes in the aluminum skin somewhere on our wings or fuselage.

The tail gunner yelled another warning and I watched two more little gray fighters zoom underneath us, one following the other. They were attacking us right through their own flak barrage! German fighters never did that. But they were.

Sometime during that wild melee I saw the bombs start to leave the belly of the lead plane. They fell in slow-motion, seeming to hang under the plane as if they were in no hurry to begin their downward plunge. Seconds later we were banking steeply to the right. We were no longer required to fly like tow-targets for the flak guns and I started to feel the surge of relief that always came when we were out of the target area. It was short-lived.

"Fighters, five o'clock low!" The shrill voice of the tail gunner didn't say they were attacking, but his tone left no doubt about it. The jackhammer sound of the fifties shook the airplane, drowning out the persistent roar of the engines. My hands were wrapped around the handles of the gun controls, my thumbs resting on the firing buttons. My hands were steady, not shaking at all, and I calmly looked through the optic gunsight to be sure it was on. How strange, I thought, because I was scared to death!

"Here comes one, seven o'clock low!" That sounded like Koehne, the ball turret gunner. An instant later I got my first shot at a German fighter. He came under us from the right and started a roll to the left, away from the formation. I held the firing buttons down and the chin turret came alive. The hammering of the fifties vibrated through the nose compartment and I could smell the fumes even through the oxygen mask. I kept firing long after the fighter was out of range.

The fighter I wasted my ammunition on wasn't one of the little swept-wing bullets. I saw it clearly, the radial engine and the wide tapered wing set well forward on the fuselage. It was a Focke-Wulf. The big black cross on the bottom of the wing stood out sharply when he flipped over on his back and rolled away from our formation.

I knew I hadn't hit the German. Probably didn't even come close. But my fear had turned to excitement, exhilaration. It was a very satisfying thing to be able to shoot back at something, a lot different than just riding through the flak and hoping not to get hit. But it happened so quickly. In three or four seconds the Focke-Wulf was in and out of my gunsight.

The Germans must have been waiting for us to get clear of the flak and the other fighters. We came off the target loose and strung out, and that was when they jumped us. I had no idea how many there were, but they made four or five passes at us and disappeared. Maybe some of our fighters showed up and ran them off, but I didn't see any friendlies around us.

The formation pulled back together again, nice and tight and pretty, the trademark of the Eighth Air Force. I leaned forward in the nose and tried to see if all the airplanes were still there, but I couldn't tell whether we'd lost anybody or not. We were half an hour away from Merseburg before I decided to take off my flak suit. The intercom had been quiet

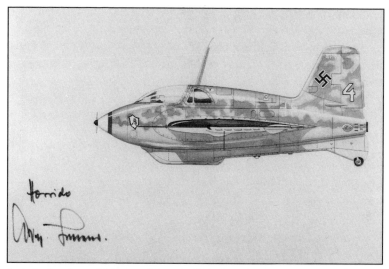

Artist's drawing of German Me-163 Komet rocket-powered aircraft, auto-graphed by Luftwaffe General Adolf Galland.

except for me calling for an oxygen check about every ten minutes. Fi-nally somebody broke the silence. "What kind of fighters were those?"

"Focke-Wulfs. Didn't you take Aircraft Recognition?"

"Hell, I don't mean those. I mean the ones over the target!"

"I dunno. Some kind of jets, I guess."

"I never even saw a picture of anything like them."

"Did you ever see anything fly that fast? Damn, they were *moving!*"

Interrogation ought to be interesting, I thought to myself.

And it was indeed. We lined up for our whiskey and hot coffee and somebody made an announcement about Interrogation being delayed until some people arrived from Headquarters. In the meantime we were not to leave the Interrogation Room.

When we finally got our turn at a table there were two Intelligence Officers waiting for us. They asked just enough questions to get us started talking, then seemed satisfied to let us talk while they wrote everything down. Each of us had something to say, and our comments ranged from objective observations to excited exclamations.

"These little jobs were really fast. They came through the formation like crap through a goose!"

"Yeah, they flew straight under us. They didn't break away like fighters are supposed to."

"From the nose it looked like they didn't have any power on when they came through. When they got out ahead of us I could see bursts of smoke when they started to climb." That comment was mine, and it elicited nods from the G-2 guys as they wrote down what I said.

After they had gotten all they could from us, they told us a bit about these new weapons. They weren't jets, but rocket fighters! They were designed at Peenemünde and made by Messerschmitt, and were called the Me-163 "Komet." They were powered by liquid rocket fuel, and could fly only for nine or ten minutes under full power. But if they used their power in short bursts it was estimated they could stay in the air for more than half an hour. The Me-163 carried two 30 mm cannons, and its speed was thought to be somewhere between five and six-hundred miles an hour. "We think it's 150 miles per hour faster than any of our fighters," one of the G-2 officers said.

The interrogation session took much longer than usual. The G-2 officers wanted every scrap of information about this new German weapon. I was a bit hesitant to mention the puffs of "miniature" flak I'd seen, but finally I decided that they weren't just my imagination.

"Did anybody else see the little puffs of flak during the fighter attack? They looked to me to be half the size of regular flak bursts."

Before anybody else could verify this, one of the G-2 guys answered, "Yes, that would have been self-detonating 30 mm cannon shells from the Messerschmitts. They use a rangefinder sight, we think, and the shells are fused to explode at given ranges without contacting the target."

So it wasn't my imagination. It was pretty damned advanced technology—a plane 150 miles per hour faster than ours, cannon shells that acted like flak—and all this was directed towards killing *me*. At least that's the way I took it.

G-2 continued, "They used another tricky little weapon against you guys, too. The reason they flew straight under your formation was to launch a pair of vertical-firing rockets at you. Of course they were just hoping for a lucky hit."

I got the impression that today might have been the first time the rocket fighters had been sent up in force against a bomb group. Apparently they had been seen by our fighters several times during the past few weeks, and once or twice they had tried to make a pass at a straggling B-17 or B-24, but those were mostly practice flights. Now they were operational, and the first combat group was stationed at Merseburg.

We found out that we lost one B-17 over Merseburg. I didn't see it go down, and I don't know whether it was flak or the rocket fighters that got it; probably flak. Every plane that was over Merseburg today had its own problems, and every crew had stories to tell. But the most incredible story by far was the ordeal of a crew from the 327th Squadron. Their B-17 took a direct hit from a flak burst on the bomb run. It was a hit that should have been fatal; the burst had exploded inside the open bomb bay. But instead of becoming a giant fireball, the plane fell out of formation still in one piece. By some miracle, the bombs hadn't exploded. The right side of the bomb bay was blown completely away, bombs and all. The radio room, just aft of the bomb bay, was a shambles. The control cables to the ailerons and elevators were shot away and, a few seconds after the B-17 fell out of formation a fire had broken out in the bomb bay. Hydraulic fluid had spilled onto the catwalk and the insulation in the bomb bay was ablaze.

The ball turret gunner was killed when the flak exploded, but miraculously nobody else was hurt. The pilot, Lt. Bosko, fought the crippled plane to try to prevent it from going into a spin. The B-17 was wallowing downward at more than 2,000 feet a minute, the bomb bay was on fire, and there were still five bombs hanging from the left rack. The engineer, Pete LaFleur, grabbed a fire extinguisher and emptied it into the burning bomb bay. When it went dry he threw it through the open doors and started pulling out the burning insulation with his bare hands. While the engineer was trying to control the fire in the bomb bay, the bombardier, Staff Sergeant Jerome Charbonneau was making his way back past the flight deck. He pushed past the engineer onto the narrow catwalk, slippery with hydraulic fluid, and surveyed the situation. The arming wires had been torn loose by the explosion, and the safety covers over the fuses were beginning to spin off, leaving the contact-sensitive fuses exposed. One bomb was already fully armed and it was just a matter of minutes before all of them would be.

Charbonneau started removing the nose fuse from the armed bomb. The radio operator, Bishop Ingraham, stuck his head into the bomb bay and Charbonneau yelled instructions to him over the roar of the wind through the open bomb bay. Ingraham started removing the tail fuse and in a few minutes was joined by the waist gunner, Charles Garrison. While the three of them worked to disarm the bombs, Bosko and the copilot, Lt. Koehnert, fought the crippled plane, which seemed determined to quit flying. Finally all the bombs were disarmed, and Charbonneau used a screwdriver to trip the shackles and get rid of them. The plane was still losing altitude, but Bosko and Koehnert refused to let it quit flying. It was as if the B-17 had taken all the punishment it could and wanted to just rest on the ground.

With only partial controls, the two pilots flew the crippled plane all the way across Germany and Belgium. Halfway across the English Channel one of the gasoline tanks went dry and an engine coughed, then went dead. The copilot feathered the engine, and by the time the big prop had stopped rotating another engine coughed. The plane was just crossing the English coast when the second engine quit, and Bosko spotted an airfield just ahead. He ordered the crew to bail out, and after he circled and made sure everybody was safely out, he landed the airplane.

These guys shared the distinction of bringing back what was undoubtedly the most heavily damaged B-17 in the history of the Ninety-second. I didn't know any of that crew except Charbonneau, and had only seen him a couple of times at bombardier's briefing. Maybe I would get a chance to talk with him about it sometime. But I wondered if maybe he wouldn't care to talk about it.

The instinct for survival can make people do the impossible. It was hard to believe that those guys didn't just bail out as soon as the plane was hit. But they didn't want to be in Germany, they wanted to be in England. Their determination was almost unbelievable.

Merseburg would undoubtedly remain number one on the Target Priority list, and I probably hadn't seen the last of it. I still had fifteen missions to go, and had a sickening feeling that the Eighth would start to concentrate on that big refinery complex. I knew that any time I saw the red yarn stretched to that pin west of Leipzig my heart would skip a beat and my insides would turn over. I began to realize how our predecessors felt about Schweinfurt.

We played poker that night and talked about the mission. The comments around the table were the usual flak-story variety, and I had the feeling that we were all a little cockier than before. It was strange, I thought, that just a few hours after experiencing such fear and terror we were making smart-aleck remarks, pretending not to take today's brush with death seriously. Perhaps that was the natural reaction after surviving a day like this one.

Jack Fromkin summed up the day in a very discerning comment he made after hearing the word "incredible" for the umpteenth time: "The most incredible thing about today is the fact that we only lost two airplanes!" I couldn't have agreed more.

Today, staring through the nose as we turned toward that black hell over Merseburg, I had felt that I was probably going to get killed. This wasn't the same fear that I felt on every mission, and it wasn't the confused terror of those first few missions. It was a profound feeling of hopelessness, as if it had just dawned on me how totally vulnerable we were. And luck, whatever that was, had seemed like a nebulous and flimsy thing to get me through that awesome black gauntlet.

But the cold fear turned to excited fear, with the adrenaline racing through my body as we flew through the flak and fighters, and as soon as it was over the fear became exhilaration. And now I was making wisecracks about it across the poker table. But in the back of my mind there was, for the first time, a little doubt about whether I could do this fifteen more times. Merseburg put it there.

TWELVE

"... WEATHER PERMITTING"

Briefing was early on August 26, with a good part of it taken up by the weather officer. He talked about low-pressure systems and occluded fronts and other things that only another weatherman could understand fully. I assumed that he was trying to tell us that we might or might not be able to get to the Primary today, so I sat there half-listening and meditating about my good fortune.

I had survived the mess over Merseburg, the flak and rocket fighters and fear. Yesterday I hadn't been alerted for the mission, but the Group went to Peenemünde and lost four B-17s. So the mission today certainly wouldn't be any worse than the last two. And from what the weather officer was saying, there was no more than a fifty-fifty chance of our going, anyway.

We were targeted for the Ruhr. Although I hadn't been there yet, I knew that the Ruhr Valley contained probably the most industrial cities in one compact group to be found in Germany. The biggest city in the valley was Düsseldorf, at the southern end. North of Düsseldorf was a gaggle of prime targets, closely packed together—Wuppertal, Essen, Oberhausen, Dortmund, and a dozen smaller cities. The Ruhr was the heart of the German iron and steel industry, but we were going after an oil refinery at the north end of the valley, at a place called Gelsen-kirchen.

The Germans were not unaware of the close proximity of these potential targets, and had provided an abundance of flak batteries to defend them. Combat flyers referred to the Ruhr by a familiar but certainly not affectionate nickname: Flak Alley.

Uncertain weather notwithstanding, we did go. The plan was to attack Gelsenkirchen from the north, and our briefed route took us over northern Belgium and southern Holland. As always I peered through the nose cone and saw absolutely nothing of the ground below. But the clouds—I had never seen such awesome masses of towering cumulus structures, rising to forty or fifty thousand feet. To avoid flying through these gigantic cloud formations, we made constant course corrections, and I had no idea where we were. I assumed that we were just flying by the seat of our pants, trying to find a way through this maze of white.

I wasn't aware that we were still climbing until I started to get unusually cold. I wondered if my heated suit was still operating and took off a glove to feel it. It was warm to the touch. I pulled the glove back on and glanced at my panel to the left. The altimeter showed 31,000! No wonder I was cold. We had been briefed for 27,000.

I alternated between watching the huge mountains of clouds that surrounded us and checking the altimeter. We were just under 32,000 when I felt a sharp pain in my left knee. I rubbed it and flexed my leg for awhile, but the pain wouldn't go away. It didn't seem to get any worse, but neither would it abate. I looked at the altimeter and we were at 32,200 feet. It dawned on me that I had the "bends." I remembered a couple of times in the pressure chamber during training when most of us got a taste of this phenomenon, and a lecture about it from the instructor. If my memory was accurate, this was caused by the formation of nitrogen bubbles in the bloodstream and only occurred at altitudes above 30,000 feet.

I had never expected to experience this in a B-17. I hadn't realized we could get that high in a loaded B-17! I watched the other planes in the formation and they were sliding back and forth a bit, just mushing along through the thin air. It was obvious that we were at absolute maximum; I don't think we could have climbed another foot. I watched the wavering planes around us and felt our own plane rising and falling slightly, or slipping a little from side to side, like a drunk trying to walk a straight line. The controls must have felt as limp as a dishrag.

I called for oxygen checks every five to ten minutes and tried to estimate how far above the cloud deck we were—no more than a few hundred feet, I surmised. We were flying along an aerial valley, between towering mountains of clouds on either side. I was miserably cold, my knee felt like somebody had jabbed it with an ice pick, and I was pessimistic about our chances of getting credit for a mission today. I expected to hear the pilot's voice on the intercom announcing that we had been recalled. The only positive thought that came to mind was that at this altitude the flak probably couldn't get us.

That was absolutely wrong. The first flak we saw was four desultory puffs at about two o'clock high! So much for that theory.

The welcoming flak bursts took my mind off the pain in my knee, and by the time I thought about it again I realized the pain was gone. I looked at the altimeter and it was unwinding slowly. We were just over 29,000 and still slowly descending. We were still surrounded by cloud formations, but they were broken, and the deck below us was thin enough so that I could occasionally see the pattern of ground below.

We were down to 28,000 when the lead plane's door started to open, and a few minutes later we dropped our bombs—visually! I could hardly believe it. A few minutes ago we were groping blindly through canyons of clouds, barely able to hold a semblance of formation in the thin air. Now here we were in our natural environment, surrounded by flak bursts and leaving a target burning below us. Some job of navigating, that was!

I don't think anybody knew it was going to turn out this way. I believe we just lucked out. Most of the groups had been recalled, and I wasn't so sure that maybe we hadn't received a recall and the C.O. had just ignored it and kept trying to find Gelsenkirchen. In any event, judging from the pyres of black smoke rising beneath us, we reduced production at the Buer Refineries.

We didn't get away from Gelsenkirchen unscathed. Just as our bomb bay doors were closing we took a hit in the number one engine. The plane staggered as if hit with a giant hammer. The sound of the explosion wasn't at all like the distant "pop" of a close burst. I grabbed my parachute pack and fumbled with the shoulder of my flak suit, trying to get out of the cumbersome armor. As the flak suit dropped to the floor I watched the prop on number one slowly wind down and stop. It was feathered and I didn't see any fire, only a little smoke. The copilot's voice sounded normal over the intercom: "Number one feathered—everybody OK?

Gelsenkirchen was number twenty-one for me. I entered it in my log with great satisfaction, noting that we lost an engine over the target. The official Group record described the mission as "difficult" and "hazardous." It was both.

I predicted we'd go on stand-down for the next few days. The weather was lousy and unpredictable, and the Group had been to three tough German targets in a row, so there were lots of holes to be patched and engines to be changed. The five B-17s that were shot down had to be replaced too. It was definitely time for a breather.

The Brass at High Wycombe felt otherwise, however, and sent down the order for a mission on the twenty-seventh. The Eighth got 1,200 bombers in the air but they did little more than form up into groups and wander around over north Germany before being recalled. Less than two hundred planes bombed targets, and none of them bombed their briefed Primary. We were among the few groups to find a target: Wilhemshaven. We encountered the same huge buildups of clouds we had wandered around in yesterday while we searched for the Ruhr, but this time we didn't have to set an altitude record. Nor did we set a record for number of planes sent out, either; we managed only to put about thirty B-17s over Wilhelmshaven.

The stand-down that I had predicted started on August 28. I figured it would last a while so I put in for another pass, as did a lot of others. Jack wanted to go to Sheffield, although I didn't know why, and he began pestering me to go along. I finally agreed that *if* our passes were approved I'd go there with him. I did this to shut him up; I didn't think I would get a pass, since it had only been a week since I'd gone to London.

Apparently the stand-down was going to last a while because there was a mass exodus of combat crews leaving the base, including me. I wondered if they kept enough people to fly the weather ship.

At Wellingborough station, Jack and I were almost alone on the northbound platform. Jack kept talking about how great Sheffield was. His information was based on what a couple of guys had told him.

Actually, Sheffield wasn't so bad. It was an industrial city, and didn't have any of the attractions London had. But it was pleasant and somehow seemed removed from the war. In London there was a vitality that could be felt almost physically, and it was a wartime vitality. Sheffield was red-brick buildings and factories with tall chimneys and there were no barrage balloons or antiaircraft guns in the parks. For that matter, there were no parks.

We checked into an old hotel right in the middle of downtown Sheffield, and had no trouble getting a room. It dawned on me as we were signing the register that I hadn't seen many uniforms, except for policemen and postmen and a couple of British soldiers. There were no Americans at all. London would be jammed with Americans, with the whole Eighth Air Force on stand-down. Maybe Sheffield wasn't such a bad idea after all.

We spent the rest of the morning walking and looking. We weren't gawking at the sights, as I always did in London, because there were really no sights to gawk at, just brick buildings, and factories, and rows of apartments, all looking very much alike and all very plain and ordinary. None of the buildings were decorated with stone carvings of lions or gargoyles, and the doorways didn't have elaborate brass doorknockers. Sheffield was the epitome of an industrial city, as different from London as night is from day.

But it did have girls—lots of girls. Noontime brought them out of the buildings and onto the sidewalks, in groups of two or three or half a dozen. I had never seen so many girls, and so few guys, in my life. Jack and I came to life, like bird dogs suddenly surrounded by coveys of quail. We looked them over carefully, smiling and nodding and occasionally saying hello. And they looked us over in the same way, making no attempt to hide their curiosity about the two American fliers. Most of them seemed very interested and very available, it was just a matter of picking out the ones we wanted to make a pass at.

I wasn't sure whether we picked them or they picked us, but we found ourselves talking with two girls who were waiting at a bus stop. They were standing away from the queue giving us the eye as we walked by, so we stopped. In a matter of minutes we found out that their names were Virginia and Mary, they worked in the same office, and they were on their lunch hour. The bus they were going to take had come and gone, and Jack and I were still trying to get them to take the rest of the afternoon off, which they said they couldn't do. We insisted on taking them to lunch, and they led us to a crowded, unpretentious little restaurant where we spent most of an hour getting to know one another and making plans for the evening. I wound up with Mary, whether by accident or intent. She was a pretty brunette, just slightly on the chubby side with a quick sense of humor and a wholesomeness that could be described as "the girl next door" type. Jack's girl was sandy-haired and wore lots of makeup. Her skirt was a good bit shorter than Mary's and I figured he might have the better deal, but I was more comfortable with Mary.

We agreed to meet at Mary's house at six o'clock. She made sure I wrote down her address, which I dutifully added to my ever-present little leather book: Mary Thorne, 217 Handsworth Road, Sheffield 9.

The girls returned to work, and Jack and I spent the afternoon seeing some things they had suggested. The only really interesting sight was the old medieval cathedral, which had been badly damaged by German bombers. During our tour it became apparent that the city had taken a good hammering from the Luftwaffe. Although it didn't seem as heavily hit as London, there was ample evidence that the German bombers had visited the city frequently.

I had some misgivings about meeting Mary's parents. They might not care for Americans, particularly one who was taking their daughter out to do whatever Americans do to English girls. But they were most cordial, and pleased to have me visit their home. It was the first time I had been inside a private home in England, and I enjoyed talking with them, telling them all about Texas and my impressions of England. The father left about seven to go to work in a steel plant, and Mary's mother, a plump, pleasant woman who reminded me somewhat of my own mother, invited us to come back later in the evening. She said there really wasn't much nightlife in Sheffield but we'd be welcome to play the phonograph and dance if we liked. She assured me it would be no bother. "I shall be asleep upstairs by ten-thirty and my 'usband won't be 'ome from work 'til morning."

As we left I thanked her for being so kind, and she gave me a hug and repeated the offer to come back later—which I had no intention of doing. But that, in fact, was exactly what we did. There really was *nothing* to do in Sheffield, except have dinner and go to the cinema, and none of us wanted to see a movie. So we spent most of the evening listening to American music on Mary's phonograph, sipping Scotch, dancing, and necking on the sofa. Jack never stopped trying to get his girl to go back to the hotel with him, but with no success. I was rooting him on, hoping to get the two of them out of there so that Mary and I could be alone, but it never happened. It was just as well, probably, because I had an uneasy feeling that if I got really intimate with Mary, her mother would appear on the stairs.

We left about two in the morning, Jack walking in a zombie-like trance as he always did when he'd had too much to drink. I promised Mary I'd write—absolutely, for sure. Just the way I'd promised the girl from Stoke-on-Trent and the little W.A.A.F. from Shropshire.

The most thrilling thing that happened all during the next day was our trying to spot the church with the Crooked Spire from the train window. It was in Nottingham, I think. Jack finally pointed it out to me, and I responded with a total lack of enthusiasm, "Yeah, Jack, great! It sure is crooked, all right." That boring trip to Sheffield reinforced my determination to never, ever waste another two-day pass.

The Liberty Run truck from Wellingborough station was filled with guys who'd been to London. The fellow sitting across from us asked if we were on the train from London. Jack said, "No, we've been in Sheffield."

"What the hell's in Sheffield?"

Jack didn't answer right away, so I did. "Great town. You oughta go there sometime!"

I don't think he caught the sarcasm, but Jack did. He gave me a disgusted look, and I said, "Isn't that right, Jack?"

Life at the Ninety-second turned out to be just as dull as my trip to Sheffield. It was September 4, and there hadn't been a plane taxied off a hardstand since August 27. The big news was the Liberation of Paris. The newsreels at the base theater were filled with footage of the Allied armies marching down the Champs Elysees and the exultation of the Parisians who showered our tanks with flowers and handed bottles of champagne to the grinning Infantrymen. Once clear of Normandy our armies had stormed across France in a matter of days, and there was general optimism about an early end to the war.

When I had first heard the news of the Invasion I had worried that the war might end too soon, before I got into it. Now, almost three months and twenty-two combat missions later, I was willing for it to end tomorrow. I would gladly relinquish the "glamour" of climbing into the nose of a B-17 and flying 500 miles to a place where a determined enemy would try everything possible to blow it out of the sky.

I went back to work on September 5. The weather was still uncertain. Lousy is a better word. But our ability to bomb accurately through cloud cover had reached the point that not even a solid overcast could prevent our nailing a target. PFF, better known by the nickname "Mickey," utilized a radar dome in the lead plane. This dome replaced the ball turret, and could be retracted into the fuselage for takeoff and landing. In the air it extended well below the belly of the plane. Some of the bombardiers had been trained to use this technique, and in my conversations with a couple of them I learned that there was a knack to reading the radar scope and identifying what you were looking at. Apparently some people had a built-in sense for reading the blips and complex light images, while others just couldn't make heads or tails of it. The only way to find out if a bombardier was a good "Mickey man" was to look at the recon photographs of the strike and see if he'd put the bombs on the M.P.I. Apparently we had some experts in the Ninety-second, and were confident about attacking any target using PFF technique.

The weather still controlled our operations, however. While we could take off in fog or overcast, if the field was socked in we couldn't land. So the determining factor in flying a mission or scrubbing it was whether we'd have a place to return to after the mission.

Today we were going after an oil refinery complex at Ludwigshafen. The target was very heavily defended, according to G-2, and we could expect to encounter intense flak. He pointed out that we could take no comfort in the fact that the flak gunners couldn't *see* us through the overcast. The batteries were radar-controlled, and the Germans were very adept in the use of gun-laying radar. "However," the G-2 officer continued, "we do have a counter-measure that seems to be proving effective—the distribution of chaff over a target." He explained that the RAF had developed the technique of blanketing a target with millions of tiny strips of metal foil, which showed up on the German radar scopes like a snowstorm, making it difficult if not impossible to detect airplanes in this sea of metal.

I was not unfamiliar with what he was describing. For some time now we had been experimenting with this technique. The window on the left side of the radio room had been replaced in many of our B-17s with a metal cover which had a rear-facing opening. During the bomb run, the radio operator heaved out packages of foil strips, one after the other, until the sky over the target area was virtually saturated with tiny strips that floated in the wind like a metal shield.

This was the first time I had heard anything about any kind of defense against flak. I thought it was about time. The constant admonitions to the gunners about fighters hadn't diminished, but the incidence of fighter attacks had. It was obvious that antiaircraft fire was the greatest hazard to our bombers. Germany reportedly had two million people assigned to flak defense. Many vital targets were surrounded by a thousand guns, arranged in *grossbatteries* of as many as twenty-seven guns tied in to a sophisticated radar gun-laying system.

The G-2 officer stopped short of saying that the tinfoil canopy would solve the problem. I didn't think it would, either, but at least it was something. I was ready to cling to anything that promised to reduce the amount or the accuracy of those terrible black bursts that made wreckage of our airplanes, and our nerves!

We were over Ludwigshafen at 27,000 feet just before noon, and they were shooting the hell out of us. We plowed through the box barrage with a sort of arrogance, as if the flak just didn't exist. From our position at the right rear of the formation I could watch the other five B-17s and occasionally I saw a plane wobble slightly from a close burst. I looked from one plane to another, tense with anxiety, expecting to see one of them blow up and trying to prepare myself for the sight. Then the "pop" of a close burst made me duck involuntarily, and reminded me that *we* might be the ones who blew up.

The knot in my stomach didn't go away. This wasn't like Merseburg, with all hell breaking loose and everything happening at once. Today it was like a slow-motion film that ground on endlessly, and I watched the flak bursts blossom as I tried to squeeze myself inside the flak suit. We came off the target with some damage to the airplane that seemed to concern the pilot. The waist gunner reported that there was a piece of metal flapping on top of the right wing between number three and four engines.

"Pilot to waist, are we losing any fuel?"

"Not that I can see. Just a loose piece of aluminum about three feet forward of the trailing edge."

The pilot sent the engineer back to the waist window to have a better look, and after a while they decided it wasn't anything to worry about. All four engines were running and we weren't on fire.

We found out when we got back to our hardstand that we were

indeed nine very lucky bastards. An 88 mm shell had torn completely through the wing just behind the main spar. It didn't explode, at least not inside the wing. The fuses were set to explode at a given altitude, not on contact, and this one exploded somewhere above us after it went through our wing. We hardly even lost any fuel; the self-sealing tanks worked just like they were supposed to.

For some reason I didn't feel the exhilaration I usually felt after getting through another rough one. I suppose I would describe today as a sobering experience for me.

The truck pulled onto the hardstand and the driver got out and waited for us to get all our gear on board. He was holding a steel helmet and as two or three of us heaved our gear over the tailgate he held it out and said, "Take a look at this thing!" He was holding it upside down. I took it from him, and turned it over. As I did a leather flying helmet fell out and I saw a ragged gash along the top of the steel pot. I reached down and picked up the leather helmet, and it was also gashed along the top. Inside, the soft chamois lining was matted with a large splotch of blood and hair.

I wanted to throw up. One of the gunners said, "Jesus Christ!" I put the leather helmet back into the steel pot and handed it back to the truck driver.

"Where did you get this?"

"Crew from 804-sugar left it in the truck. One of their gunners. He's still alive, too. They've got him in the radio room—the flight surgeon's working on him right now."

When I entered Ludwigshafen in my log book, I added the notation, "BLOODY!!!!"

I sat for awhile and studied the little log book, and for the first time noticed how it had changed. The first page was filled with precise, neatly printed entries, written by someone who savored each of these victories. The second page started out in the same style, but gradually the printing became less precise, printed hastily, as if the writer wanted to get it over with. There were blots where the book had been closed before the ink had time to dry. The comments on the facing page, cryptic notes that reflected my mood immediately after each mission, referred to losses, or fear, or the horror of something I'd seen.

The log book was an accurate mirror of my feeling about combat flying. It was very obvious halfway through the second page that my cocky period was coming to an end. The excitement, the feeling that each mission was a great adventure, had been replaced by a seriousness that hadn't been there before. I wondered whether the missions were really getting tougher, or whether they were just getting to me. Was Merseburg really that much worse than Munich, or Hamburg? Had I flinched at the sound of a flak burst over Leipzig the way I did today over Ludwigshafen? All I really knew was that I had to do it twelve more times, and I felt certain I could do it.

Pretty certain, anyway.

THIRTEEN

WAITING GAME

September was the month when I expected to come close to finishing my combat tour. I had flown ten missions in August, and if I could repeat that in September I'd be down to two.

A two-day stand-down followed the Ludwigshafen raid. My jitters had abated and I was anxious to get on with it. The battle damage reports confirmed what I had felt about the mission, and eased my mind about my being so jumpy. It had definitely been tougher. Most of our B-17s had been severely damaged, and it took two days to get them ready to fly again. They flew again on the eighth, but my name wasn't on the Alert List. They went back to Ludwigshafen and hit the same target, the huge I. G. Farben Industrie synthetic oil complex. This time the flak gunners got one. A Fort from the 325th Squadron took a direct hit and dived out of formation in flames. The crew bailed out, unfortunately, because the pilot managed to get the plane to France and to crash-land it in friendly territory.

There was a mission to Mannheim on the ninth and Sindelfingen on the tenth, and I wasn't alerted for either of them. I was beginning to get the feeling again that they had misplaced my name somewhere in the files.

The mission to Sindelfingen on the tenth resulted in the loss of a 326th crew to German flak batteries. Spencer was the pilot. I had a casual acquaintance with him and several of the crew members. One of the gunners on the crew was an energetic, effervescent little guy named Jack Spratt. I met him in the equipment room a couple of missions earlier, and thought he was kidding when he told me what his name was. I was sorry to hear that this smiling, happy-go-lucky fellow and his crew were shot down.

But as it turned out, this loss was only temporary. Two days later Jack, Spencer, and the other seven guys landed back at the Group. Not in their B-17, of course; it was totaled by flak and had crashed somewhere in France, near the German border—after the crew had bailed out. Spencer and his guys stepped out of General George Patton's personal C-47 like conquering heroes, carrying bottles of French champagne and wearing Bronze Stars pinned to their flight suits. They were also wearing big smiles.

What had happened to them was almost unbelieveable. Their Fort was shot all to hell, and dropped out of formation, but Spencer and the copilot fought it for as long as they could, keeping it barely flying and headed west, out of Germany. Finally they had no choice but to jump; the plane just wouldn't fly any longer. The navigator was certain they were still in enemy territory, but the plane would go no further, so they hit the silk.

After they landed and got together, discussing what to do next and still certain they were behind enemy lines, they saw what appeared to be an American Army vehicle. It was olive drab and had a white star on the side. It turned out that they had jumped right into the forward element of General Patton's Third Army.

They were taken to the general's headquarters tent at Châlons-sur-Marne, happy to be alive and happier yet to be in non-German hands. They expected a routine interrogation by somebody in Patton's HQ, but in a few minutes the gun-toting general himself arrived. He greeted them and offered congratulations on their escape from disaster. The whole thing was a little stiff and formal until Jack Spratt pulled out his "short-snorter" bill and asked, with a big grin, "General, would you sign my short-snorter, sir?" Patton grinned back and said Hell yes, he'd be happy to. He ordered some champagne brought in to celebrate the crew's efforts, then out of the blue turned to a colonel and said, "Get me nine Bronze Stars for these men." Patton personally pinned the medal on each man, and they had another round of champagne.

As it turned out, the general had screwed up. When they got off Patton's plane back at the Ninety-second, the Awards and Decorations Officer asked Spencer what the hell they were wearing. Spencer said it was obvious; they were wearing Bronze Stars, and furthermore, they had been pinned on by old Blood-and-Guts personally. The awards officer pointed out that it was against all regulations to award the Bronze Star for any aerial operation. Spencer then pointed out that Patton was wearing four stars and the awards officer had only a gold leaf, so he and his guys weren't about to give up their medals.

Colonel Moose Hardin, our Squadron C.O., inherited the impasse and it was up to him either to tell General Patton he had screwed up, or else figure some way out of this breach of regulations. Moose, naturally, figured a way out. What he did was to cut orders assigning Spencer and his crew to temporary duty with the Third Army at Châlons-sur-Marne. The orders were pre-dated and covered the period September 10, 1944, to September 12, 1944, so technically Spencer and his guys were attached to the Third Army when the award was made. This made everything legal. The crew kept their Bronze Stars and their photographs taken with General Patton, finished the case of champagne he sent back with them, and lived happily ever after. So far as I know, anyway.

There was a Maximum Effort Alert posted for the eleventh, and I wasn't on that one, either. My hopes for finishing in September were fading rapidly. The month was one-third gone and I'd only flown one mission. I cursed my luck, but the next morning I happily pulled the covers over my head and stayed in the sack while the other guys bitched and moaned and trudged out into the 3 a.m. chill. I sent them off with a satisfied, "Turn out the lights when you leave!"

I was sitting in the reading room at the club that afternoon when I heard the planes coming back. I put down the magazine and walked outside as the first squadron wheeled over the runway and three B-17s peeled off. I decided to walk on down in the direction of the control tower and watch them come in. By the time I was halfway there a couple of more squadrons had come over the field. There didn't seem to be enough airplanes. Maybe there was another squadron yet to come.

By the time I got to the tower I had a feeling that we'd had a bad time that day. And I was right. I heard somebody say, "They caught it today. The 407th got wiped out!"

"What the hell do you mean, wiped out?"

"That's what I heard. They lost the whole damn squadron!"

I had a gut feeling where they'd been, but I asked anyway. They'd been to Merseburg.

Everything had gone wrong at Merseburg. The first bomb run was aborted and the Group made a three-sixty and started a second run. They ran into a tremendous flak barrage and the formation became loose and scattered. Just at bombs-away fifteen Focke-Wulfs and Messerschmitts came out of nowhere and made a determined attack on the lead element. Between the flak and the fighter attack, twelve B-17s went down. Twelve!

The 407th took the heaviest losses. They weren't wiped out, but close to it. Actually, four of the planes that were hit made it back as far as France or Belgium and either crash-landed or the crews bailed out. We didn't lose twelve crews, thank God, but we lost twelve airplanes, and almost eighty men were either dead or down somewhere in Germany.

I'd had a terrible feeling about Merseburg after my trip there in August, and today's disaster convinced me that it was the worst place in Germany to be caught in a B-17. That night in the combat mess all the talk was about Merseburg. Somebody said they had a big gunnery school there, and that's why the flak was so accurate. Another guy said, "Yeah, I understand you've gotta be at least a staff sergeant to be assigned to a flak battery at Merseburg." Wisecracks, always wisecracks. But why not? It would be very easy to become depressed after a day like this, and perhaps the wisecracks kept us from doing that.

The Group didn't fly another mission until the seventeenth, and I missed that one, too. It was one I would really like to have made. We bombed a big installation of flak batteries in North Holland. It was a tactical mission for a big invasion, an airborne attack that was going to shorten the war. The BBC War News was giving it as much coverage as D-Day in Normandy. A combined force of British and American airborne troops were dropped at three strategic towns, Eindhoven, Nijmegen, and Arnhem. According to General Montgomery, this was the shortest route to Berlin. The idea was to capture and hold the bridges in these towns so that American and British armored divisions could race toward the heart of the Third Reich. It was a bold stroke, according to *Stars and Stripes* and the BBC, and the more I heard about it, the more I felt cheated in not being involved in our support strike. I thought that most of all I would love to have dumped some bombs on the German flak batteries.

The morning of the nineteenth I walked into the squadron office and put in for a two-day pass to London. I was feeling belligerent; the Group had gone out this morning and once again I wasn't alerted. I was frustrated to the point of anger, and if I'd gotten any argument over asking for another pass I was ready to point out that I was a combat flyer and I hadn't been off the ground in two weeks.

The pass was no problem. The Group was on stand-down for the next two days and I signed out early on the twentieth and caught the nine-twenty from Wellingborough. My friend George greeted me in the lobby of the Winston and walked with me to the receptions counter. I signed the register under an entry that caught my interest. It was for a flight officer, and the name was followed by the initials "D.F.C." I commented on this to George as we walked back to his desk. "That's customary, actually," he said. "The RAF doesn't 'and them out freely—not atall." The U.S. Army Air Corps does, I thought to myself, and I didn't think I'd have the nerve to sign it after my name.

I stashed my things in a neat little room not much bigger than a closet and headed down to the l'Auberge de France to see if Kay was still there. I didn't see her, so I asked the lady in charge if Kay still worked in the restaurant. She said, "She does indeed, but today she reports to work at two." I thanked her and started to leave, but she asked me where I was from and we wound up in a nice conversation. She was the most typically British lady I'd seen. She was in her fifties and had a very aristocratic air. She wore tailored suits and a pince-nez, and her gray hair was pulled back in a tight bun. She seldom smiled, and I think Kay was afraid of her.

There was nobody in the restaurant. We talked for awhile, and she invited me to make myself at home. I wound up playing some boogie-woogie on the grand piano by the window. She brought tea for the two of us and asked if I could play anything besides the rambunctious music I was pounding out. I really couldn't; I'd learned boogie-woogie from records and played strictly by ear. But I did know a few other songs, and started one called "In a Country Garden." She smiled broadly and said, "Oh, not Percy Grainger—you needn't go that far!"

I felt that I was beginning to understand the English people. They seemed at first to be somewhat cold and aloof. They were polite but very formal, and most Americans took this as being unfriendly. But I had no trouble at all in getting to know them, and found them very warm and friendly. And with most of them, just underneath that shell of proper manners lurked a dry sense of humor that very often was directed toward themselves. It was like a cartoon I saw in *Punch* that showed a

Spitfire pilot standing beside his plane, which was riddled with holes, and the intelligence officer with his clipboard was saying, "Modesty is one thing, Lieutenant, but saying 'nothing to report' is carrying it a bit far!"

The first time I saw Barbara was on a sidewalk near Marble Arch. She and two other A.T.S. girls had just left a restaurant and were talking as I approached them. Her two companions said "see you later" or something like that, and left just as I arrived. Barbara looked at her wristwatch and when she looked up I said, "Hi there." She smiled and said "Hello."

She was a very, very pretty girl, even in the brown wool uniform. She was a private in the British equivalent of our Women's Army Corps, and her cap had the insignia of the Royal Artillery on it. I guessed she was about twenty, perhaps only nineteen. She was about five-feet-two, trim, brown-eyed, and I hoped to hell she didn't say she had to meet somebody else.

We walked along in the direction of Hyde Park, and our conversation was very relaxed and comfortable. I wasn't giving her a line, and she wasn't being coy. We just talked. She insisted on calling me "Freddie," which I didn't particularly mind. Nobody else called me that, but it sounded very natural the way she said it.

I said, "I really wasn't out to pick up a girl—not until I saw you, anyway."

She laughed and said something to the effect that I probably said that to all the girls.

She was from Surrey and had been in the Royal Artillery for two years. She said she had been stationed at Dulwich most of the time, and probably would stay there. I asked why, and she explained, "The buzz bombs, you know. They come right over Dulwich and we try to shoot them down before they get to London."

"My God, you're a flak gunner!"

She really laughed this time, a genuine laugh, not a girlish giggle. "I expect you're not especially fond of flak, are you?"

"Not especially—and I just missed a chance to bomb some flak batteries in Holland. I don't usually care if I miss a mission, but I really wish I'd been out on that one."

By late afternoon Barbara and I were as comfortable together as if we'd known each other for years. (I had forgotten all about Kay.) She was very straightforward and open, not at all coquettish. And I wasn't using the lines or making the innuendos that I often did with girls. It wouldn't have worked with Barbara, not a chance. I really liked her, and enjoyed being with her. And I knew very well I wasn't going to get her in the sack—not right now, maybe never.

She had to be back at her station and sign in by midnight, so I offered to ride with her from Victoria station to Dulwich. She insisted that wasn't necessary, and I'd have to come back to London by myself. But she didn't insist too strenuously, and I wasn't anxious for us to part company. So we took the train to Dulwich, and walked alongside a stone wall that never seemed to end until finally we were at the main gate to her base. She didn't seem anxious for us to part company either. She asked very matter-of-factly, "Will I see you again?"

"You darn sure will, any time I can get to London!"

"You have my number, so try to give me a ring before you come. I can usually get away for a day—change duty with one of the girls." As an afterthought she added, "Let me give you my parents' number. They always know where I am, in the event you can't get through to me here."

"But they're in Surrey. Where is Surrey, anyway?"

She laughed and pointed down the road, "Just there, right on the edge of London, really."

I walked back to the station at Dulwich and sat down to wait for the train back to London. I lit a cigarette and took out my little book to double-check Barbara's address. It was on the first page; when I opened the book and handed her my fountain pen, she said something about this being the first page and I said, "Yes, I've been saving it just for you!"

She had written, very precisely, everything I needed to know . . . W/81637 Pte. Hardin, B., 427 H.A.A. Bty. R.A., Grange Lane, College Road, Dulwich S.E. 21, Phone TERminus-7049. It looked very military; in fact, the printing was similar to my own. But underneath she signed her name, as if she were autographing the page. And that didn't look military at all. This was the fourth English girl I'd promised to write, or call, or see again. This time I would, I was sure of that.

My name finally appeared on an Alert List, and it appeared to be a Maximum Effort. Wake up call was early on the twenty-second, and the fuel load was maximum. I wasn't expecting a short trip anyway, and certainly there wouldn't be any more milk runs to France. We occupied France now, so there were no Germans left to bomb. All I wanted was to log another mission. I hadn't been inside a B-17 in *seventeen* days.

We were briefed for a PFF bomb run, which I expected, because the weather showed no signs of improving. Our target was at Kassel, about halfway across Germany. The big Henschel plant there was one of the largest armored vehicle factories in Germany, large enough that we should be able to hit it whether we could see it or not.

The name was familiar to me. I remembered reading about Henschel airplanes back in the thirties. Maybe they weren't making planes any more, just tanks. I was feeling more like my old self, not particularly jumpy and with no feeling of impending doom.

When it was over the flak over Kassel was probably classified as "moderate" by G-2 and in fact we lost a B-17 over the target. But battle damage was fairly light and for some reason I added the notation "milk run" when I logged this one. Kassel didn't qualify as a milk run, but I decided that my log was beginning to read a little too much like a horror story.

One fairly nice September afternoon (it was not raining) I got on my bike and rode around the air base, going nowhere in particular. I found myself on the opposite side of the perimeter track near hangar number two, and decided since I hadn't been inside it I'd kill a little time browsing around inside, looking at the shot-up B-17s.

Parked in a corner of the hangar was a dusty-looking B-17, still in the old camouflage paint, that had a strange look about it. I walked closer and saw that it had a chin turret, so I assumed it was a late "F" or a "G" model. I walked around the airplane and noticed the guns. It bristled with caliber-fifties. I counted fourteen machine guns. Ours only had ten. This thing had two upper turrets, one in the current standard position just behind the flight deck and another just behind the radio room. And the waist guns were pairs rather than single guns.

Thinking I had stumbled onto a secret airplane of some kind, I waited until a crew chief detached himself from a group of mechanics and approached him. I said, "Chief, is this something I'm not supposed to see?"

He laughed and replied, "That thing's been sitting there for a year. Look her over all you want!"

"What the hell is it, anyway?"

"That there's a YB-40. It was called a 'Heavy Formation Defense Airplane,' I think."

"What was it supposed to do?"

"It was a brainstorm of Colonel Keck and Colonel Reed's. They were Majors then, back in the spring of 1943. You see, there wasn't any fighter escort that could go all the way to the target and back and the German fighters were having a field day with the B-17s after the fighters turned back. This YB-40 was supposed to give protection to the formation all the way to the target and back."

"Did it work?"

"Well, yes and no. It's got plenty of firepower; you can see that. And it carried about 12,000 rounds of caliber-fifty ammo. And it's got lots of armor. Almost all the gun positions have got half-inch armor plate around them. But it couldn't keep up with the bombers on the way back." He went on to explain that this monster weighed about the same as a loaded B-17. But after the bombs are dropped, the B-17s could just head for home, while the YB-40s, just as heavy as when they took off, couldn't keep pace.

"Did the other groups have these too? I never even heard about them."

"Just the Ninety-second. In fact, just the 327th Squadron."

Apparently there were only a few of these made; perhaps a dozen, perhaps not that many. They started flying in the late spring of 1943, but by fall they had been outmoded by long-range P-51s and P-47s. While the YB-40 wasn't a success, as such, something good did come out of it: the chin turret. Up until then the nose gun was a single hand-operated *caliber-thirty* that stuck through the Plexiglas, and that little peashooter didn't do much to dissuade German fighters. They would come through the formation from the front, spread out in what the combat crews called a "company front" attack, and when they flew through a formation, the B-17s fell like leaves in the fall. But the two caliber-fifties in the chin turret discouraged that sort of behavior.

The YB-40 was one of the least-known airplanes ever used during the war, and the Ninety-second was the group that used them.

Another two-day stand-down didn't come as a big surprise. One of the weather officers had noted that this was the worst September weather in several years. Filling in time between missions required some creativity and a month earlier I had started studying German. I was getting pretty good at pronouncing the words, but the grammar threw me completely. Jack Fromkin, who spoke excellent German, was my unofficial tutor. During one session, with Jack asking questions from the book and me trying to come up with the answers, he said, "You know, Fred, if you're ever shot down and captured they'll probably execute you."

"Why would they do that?" I asked.

"Three reasons. First, your name is German. Second, you're the guy that actually drops the bombs. And third, you'll be speaking German with a Jewish accent."

Jack and I had gotten to be very close friends. Sometimes his moods got really black and he'd confide in me that he was thinking about quitting, just refusing to fly any more missions. I didn't think he was serious, and we'd walk over to the club and have a couple of beers or bicycle into Rushden to get away from the base. I'd reassure him that he was just reacting normally. Actually, I don't think he felt any different than I had felt at times; he just showed it more openly. And I think part of it was his position. The tail gunner's spot was a lonely, tight little place, far away from the rest of the crew. Fighter attacks usually got the tail-gunner first. There was a song about flying combat in bombers that had a chorus that ended, "Wash the tail gunner out with a hose."

Three days after the Kassel raid I flew my twenty-fifth mission. We went to Osnabrück and tore up several miles of railroad track in the marshaling yards. Osnabrück was due east of the battle zone where the airborne troops were dropped just over a week ago, and the battle was not going well. The BBC announcer's voice was somber as he referred to the "unflinching courage of the British airborne soldiers at Arnhem," but it had become apparent that they had lost this particular battle. They hadn't surrendered, not yet, but the news reports made it clear that this was inevitable.

I don't know whether our disrupting the German transportation system at Osnabrück helped them any; probably not. But it was the first time we'd bombed visually in awhile, and I got tremendous satisfaction in being able to lean forward and watch our bomb bursts as we banked away from the city.

I logged Osnabrück at the top of the third page of my log, and described it as a milk run. There were fourteen lines left on the page. More than I'd need.

The last day of September was spent flying around western Germany, just south of Osnabrück, frustrated by the weather and trying to find a decent target somewhere near our briefed Primary. The whole area was covered by a solid deck of cloud. We bombed PFF and unloaded over a hundred tons of high-explosive on Münster. The intention was to tear up some more railroad track in the central marshaling yards and switching station.

The raids on Münster and Osnabrück were strategic rather than tactical, but they produced a more immediate result than some strategic missions. Bombing a factory or an oil refinery had a definite effect on the German war effort, but it was a long-term proposition. When we tore up a railway yard, this could immediately disrupt the movement of troops and supplies to or from the battle front. To add to the Germans' woes, our fighters often followed up our strike with low-level strafing runs on individual trains, blowing up engines and wrecking tank cars or box cars.

It seemed to me that we were concentrating on targets east of the battle along the Rhine to help with the airborne invasion at Eindhoven, Nijmegen, and Arnhem. But this "bold stroke" had fizzled badly, and tragically. The British First Airborne had lost almost three-quarters of its troops to the savage German opposition. The American 101st Airborne had managed to take and hold its objective near Nijmegen, but with the Germans holding Arnhem it was a dead-end road. General Montgomery's vision of a blitzkrieg-like dash to Berlin faded into the damp September mist.

The war on the ground had slowed almost to a halt, and the air war wasn't doing much better. During the entire month of September the Ninety-second managed to put only 400 B-17s over targets. The average was thirty bombers per mission, a long way from a Maximum Effort. And our losses were the worst since April, according to official Group reports. The Luftwaffe and the flak defenses, which had been spread over all of western Europe, were now concentrated within the borders of Germany. It wasn't my imagination, the missions *were* getting tougher. The days of the occasional milk run were all but over, it appeared, and Germany was beefing up its defenses for a last stand.

My personal air war wasn't doing so hot either. I flew only four missions during September, after beginning the month with the outside hope that I might be finished, or nearly so, by the month's end. The dreary, rainy days and the stand-downs, the scrubbed missions and the gloomy news reports about the war on the ground combined to change optimism into pessimism.

The Group needed a shot of enthusiasm, and this came late in September in the form of our new commanding officer. Since August 26 our C.O., Colonel William Reid, had been laid up in the hospital. He had been hit by flak over Gelsenkirchen, a poor reward for his tenacity in leading us to our target that day when most of the Eighth Air Force had been recalled. The new C.O. was Colonel James Wilson, and he had also been wounded during his combat tour last year. Now, after spending a while in the States, he was back to take over the Ninety-second after first completing a couple of special assignments for General "Hap" Arnold.

It didn't take Colonel Wilson long to make his presence known. He had been in the Group only two days when he led us on the Münster raid. And he popped up all over the base, appearing in the most unexpected places, getting to know everything about the Ninety-second and everybody in the Group. The Colonel was quiet and unassuming, very quick to smile, and casual in his approach to us. We quickly sensed that everything about him was genuine. His enthusiasm was refreshing and his approach to commanding the Group didn't seem to involve issuing orders or raising hell about things he didn't like. He was dynamic and at the same time friendly and quiet. In short, Colonel James Wilson was a nice guy.

I wondered whether bird-colonels in the Infantry grabbed rifles and went on patrols with the squads, or led battalions up hills to take German bunkers. I doubted it. But bird-colonels in the Eighth Air Force got into B-17s and went to Germany. And they didn't just do it once in a while to make an impression; they did it regularly and routinely, and they got shot at, and sometimes hit, just like anybody else. It was just part of the job. During my three months in the Ninety-second I had seen Colonel Reid a dozen times more or less, and on all but one or two occasions he was in flying clothes, either going out on a mission or just coming back from one.

The new C.O. perked things up at the end of a dreary, unproductive month. It gave us all something to talk about, to speculate on. Even if he'd been an iron-assed S.O.B. his arrival would have provided something to bitch about, but there wasn't a single negative comment heard about Colonel Wilson. We knew instinctively that whatever he did would very likely be good for the Group, and for us. Now if he could just do something about the damn weather.

FOURTEEN

LUCK OF THE DRAW

During one of our late-night poker games in the hut, which had become more frequent as the weather kept us on the ground, Bob Danielson was having an unusually bad night. His normally sour disposition had gone from bad to worse as he drew good cards and still lost hand after hand. Finally he threw his cards onto the table and said in total disgust, "If I didn't have bad luck I wouldn't have any luck at all!"

His comment summed up exactly the way I felt about my combat flying. We were two weeks into October and I hadn't been off the ground—not once. And it wasn't because I hadn't made the Alert List. I had been to briefing three times, and three times the mission was scrubbed.

It was far more frustrating than not being alerted at all. I had gone through all the motions—the early wake up call, the miserable chill in the hut at three in the morning as I tried to get my clothes on as quickly as possible, the ritual of breakfast and briefing, the scramble in the equipment room to get suited up, the truck ride through the cold swirling fog to the hardstand. And all the while I was getting mentally prepared to go out and get shot at.

Then we'd sit in the tent by the hardstand for an hour. . . . Two hours. . . . Occasionally I'd walk over and look out and watch the rain dripping off the waiting B-17. Finally a red flare would go up and we'd wait, disgusted and wondering how we'd spend the rest of the day, for the truck to take us back to the equipment room. The mental letdown was close to depression.

As I pulled off the wet flight coveralls I'd try to tell myself that I really didn't want to be flying in weather like this, anyway. But the fact is, I did. The ritual of getting ready for a mission was like a snowball rolling downhill, faster and faster, and the end result was lifting slowly off the runway and climbing through the overcast. Stopping the process midway through seemed unnatural and I never felt relieved because I wouldn't have to go out and get shot at. I was *ready* to go out and get shot at, and to put another mission behind me.

There was no doubt in my mind that we all felt the same about scrubbed missions. The bitching had a more sincere ring to it, and the mood was one of utter frustration. My personal frustration was compounded by the fact that *sometimes* a mission actually did get off the ground, but it was one I wasn't alerted for. The Group had gone to Kassel and Nürnberg and Cologne and Zwickau, all PFF bombing and mostly not on the Primary target. We had lost two B-17s over Nürnberg, one at Cologne, and one at Zwickau, so I hadn't missed any milk runs, but I also hadn't logged any missions.

On Friday the thirteenth I put in for a pass to London. Our B-17s sat on the hardstands with the rain glistening on the polished aluminum skin and dripping from the trailing edges of the wings, forming little puddles here and there on the wet concrete. It had been raining for four days, and the gray clouds hung so low you could almost reach up and touch them. Our hut was so damp and cold that we had scrounged a supply of coke and fired up the potbellied stove. It didn't really warm the hut, but it felt good if you sat close to it.

There was supposed to be an Alert coming down by that afternoon. It was late in the day when the list was finally posted, and my name wasn't on it, so I could go. I wanted to call Barbara and let her know I was coming. I phoned later that night, after I was sure my pass was OK'ed, and spoke with a female duty sergeant. She sounded very military and not particularly friendly, but she said she would get word to Barbara that I'd be in London tomorrow. I asked her to be sure and tell Barbara to leave a message at the Winston. When I hung up I wasn't sure she'd understood me; I hadn't understood her too well.

Early Saturday morning I signed out and waited for the Liberty Run truck to Wellingborough. The rain had stopped, but the low-hanging clouds were still there, and the air felt wet. The London train was half empty and I watched the English countryside roll by, lush and green under the gray overcast, with a few fields turning tan.

It wasn't raining in London, but the streets were wet and the low clouds moved over the city like waves. Curiously, I liked the city even better in this weather. It was more like London was supposed to look. I had never pictured London as being bright and sunny, but that's the way it had been on my previous trips. The dark overcast sky and the wet streets added to the mystique of the city.

It was only eleven o'clock when I walked into the lobby of the Winston, and the rooms weren't ready yet. I left my musette bag with George, after giving him two packs of Luckies. He was cordial and happy to see me, and apologized for the weather. I asked him where I should check to see if there was a message for me, and he insisted on going to check on it. He was back momentarily and handed me a folded note. It said, "13:30 Victoria Station. B. Hardin."

I was at the right platform at Victoria, standing casually with my hands in my pockets when Barbara showed up. I said, "What's a nice girl like you doing out in weather like this?"

"Isn't it simply awful? Just doesn't let up. Have you been flying in this?"

"Not much. I think even the birds are walking."

I hailed a taxi, said "Piccadilly Circus," and we got in. Then I asked Barbara what she'd like to do. Lunch, a movie? We talked about it for a while and I suggested we spend a couple of hours at the wax museum. I asked her if she'd been to Tussaud's, and she said it had been years ago, when she was a child. She seemed to like the idea, so I told the cabbie to head for Marylebone Road instead of Piccadilly.

After Tussaud's we walked for awhile in Regent's Park, talking about everything in general. She was more interested in knowing about Texas than hearing stories about my combat flying. I asked her how flak guns worked, and she explained in considerable detail. Then she asked about my girlfriends back in the States.

Barbara was very comfortable to be with. She had an honest openness about her that made me respond the same way. I knew what her reaction would be if I played the brash, cocky American flyer with a pocketful of money, so I didn't assume that role. We didn't really talk much about my combat flying, but if she'd asked how I felt about it I would probably have confessed that it scared me to death. With other girls I would have been more likely to tell exaggerated flak stories with emphasis on my coolness under fire.

Inevitably we found ourselves in the Universelle Brasserie, mixing with the mass of humanity. It was impossible to find a spot where we could sit and have a drink and carry on a conversation, so after a while I arget area wasn't the satisfaction of having caused a lot of destruction; : was the satisfaction of survival. If my bombs landed harmlessly in an pen field I would still have felt the elation of one who has been shot at nd missed.

I didn't say any of this to Barbara, I just sat with her in the station tea hop until train time and learned how deeply she felt about the war. One hing was abundantly clear: she had never seen any glamour in it, even uring the Battle of Britain when the gallant Spitfire pilots were hurling ack the waves of German bombers. She thought the whole thing was orrible, frightening, and barbaric.

It hadn't really struck me until then that England, particularly Lon-lon, had been a battlefield for *five years*. First it was the bomber blitz. God knows how many Londoners were killed during those days. And he air raids really hadn't ever completely stopped, they had only be-ome less and less frequent as the RAF gained air superiority over the Luftwaffe. Then the buzz-bomb blitz, which began barely four months go, had already killed more than 5,000 Londoners. And waiting in the vings were the V-2s, the huge rockets that were poised deep in Ger-nany to be launched against the battered city. They were already eginning to fall on London and there was absolutely no defense gainst them. They came straight down, faster than the speed of sound, nd the tremendous explosion came without warning. Barbara's flak atteries couldn't shoot them down.

My objectives were pretty superficial, I decided, compared to Bar-ara's. I only had to finish my tour and go home. For the English, this *as* home, and the only way they could get out of the war was for it to nd.

I didn't ride the train to Dulwich. Barbara insisted it simply wasn't ecessary, and I finally agreed. I promised to call her soon and she eemed pleased. I wondered if she was going out with anyone else, but I idn't ask.

It was late Sunday afternoon when I got back to the Group, and we vere on stand-down. I could have stayed in London for another day and : wouldn't have made any difference.

fter seventeen days of inactivity I was actually wriggling through the ose hatch of a B-17. I had almost forgotten how it smelled: it had a istinctive odor of aluminum and zinc chromate, electrical wiring,

asked, "Barbara, have you had enough of this?" She sm[i]
ded, and we made our way through the crowd and up th[e]
Piccadilly sidewalk. We had dinner in the elegant, crystal-
dining room at the Regent Palace. It was leisurely, quiet, a[nd]
The service was impeccable and unhurried, and it was ver[y]
suppose she thought I was just trying to impress her; pe[r]

After dinner we walked down The Mall to St. James'[s]
for a long time on a bench. There was no moon, but Bucki[ngham]
was faintly visible. Our reverie was suddenly ended by t[he]
buzz bomb. It sounded very close and I tried to spot it. Bar[bara]
and her grip on my arm tightened. The engine cut out
hear the faint whistle of the bomb for fifteen seconds or
explosion. It wasn't far away, probably a couple of miles

After Barbara calmed down we walked on to Victoria st[ation]
out how deeply she felt about the buzz bombs. It was
although her reaction had been the same as my reaction
burst. She really hated the bombs, and the people that s
London. She seemed to feel that the Germans were inten[t]
to kill and maim as many people as possible. No doubt s[he]
wondered if the German who pushed the switch to laun[ch]
tonight was hoping to kill as many people as he could. Pe[rhaps]
particularly if he'd lost his home or seen his family k
bombs—or ours, for that matter.

I began to realize what a different perspective I had a[t]
really hadn't talked seriously to anyone who had been in t[he]
battle from the start and had a burning hatred, a desire
didn't hate the Germans. They were just the enemy and v
out a load of bombs it was with no more emotion than tryi[ng]
clay target on the skeet range. The target was only a far-a[way]
buildings and roads and checkpoints five miles below.
leaned forward to watch the bomb strike it was to see if t[he]
in the right part of that pattern. I never had any mental pic
flying through the air, or people screaming, or houses b[urning]

My emotion was not the result of destroying a ta[rget or]
people. It was the result of the target shooting back—at [me]
the flak bursts a lot more clearly than my own bombs [and]
that's what I reacted to. And my satisfaction when we

hydraulic fluid, and whatever else made a B-17 smell like that. They all smelled the same. I hadn't always flown in the same airplane, but the familiar odor made it seem like I had.

Today's strike would be PFF, according to the weather officer. We were going to tear up another railway yard, this one at Cologne. The huge Eifeltor Marshalling Yard was a vital transportation link, a main point on the Siegfried Line. Our ground troops had been up against this vaunted German defensive line for several weeks. The airborne invasion a month earlier was an attempt to make an end run around the north end of the line. That hadn't worked and our guys were going to have to go through it.

We formed up in the blue sky over the solid white mass that covered England and as soon as we left the English coast I went back and pulled the pins. Settled comfortably in my seat in the nose, my oxygen mask still cold against my face, I glanced at the altimeter when Jack announced that the Dutch coast was coming up. We were climbing through 16,000. It must have been only a few seconds later that something hit me between the shoulder blades with such force that I was knocked off my seat.

My God, I've been killed! I didn't *say* it, but I just knew it. I was absolutely numb, and I have no doubt that my heart stopped, at least momentarily. I was on my knees in front of my seat, with my hands against the Plexiglas nose cone. I have no idea how long it was before my brain started to function. It was almost like a voice telling me that I was still alive, I wasn't in pain, I could see, I was breathing.

I don't remember getting back onto my seat, but I did. I turned around and Jack was just behind me. He was holding an oxygen regulator in one hand and pointing at it with the other. I heard the pilot's voice on the intercom. "What's going on down there?"

Jack answered, "Oxygen regulator blew out. Almost salvoed our bombardier!"

"You guys all right?"

I decided I could talk now, and pressed the intercom button. "Yeah, OK, but I'm not getting any oxygen."

The regulator blow-out had emptied the system that I used. The pilot said, "Grab a walk-around bottle and go back to the Radio Room. You'll have to ride back there; there's an extra outlet."

I maneuvered through the hatch under the flight deck, holding the basketball-size oxygen bottle in front of me, and stood up behind the copilot's seat. The pilot turned around and took off his oxygen mask to yell, "I'll call the radio operator before the bomb run. You can use the bottle during the bomb run." I nodded and tiptoed along the catwalk in the bomb bay to the radio room.

I found a spot on the floor on the right side and sat down. The oxygen outlet was on the bulkhead between the radio room and the bomb bay. I disconnected from the bottle and plugged into the outlet. I looked around for a place to plug in my heated suit, but there wasn't one. The radio operator was plugged into the only outlet.

It only took a few minutes for me to realize just how much I hated being in that dim, cramped, windowless, little room. I could look straight up through the Plexiglas skylight in the roof, but all I could see was sky. Occasionally I got up into a crouching position and tried to look through the little side window, but it was tiny and needed cleaning. Jesus, how I'd like to be up there in my greenhouse seeing everything that was going on, I thought. Even if nothing was going on, I was used to being able to see the clouds, the other planes in the formation, other groups in the distance.

I watched the radioman as he fiddled with the dials on the racks of radio equipment stacked up over his table. He was busy today, monitoring "C-Channel," I thought. Occasionally he looked over and waved a gloved hand in my direction, just to let me know he knew I was there. I wondered how he could stand being cooped up in that little room, isolated and not able to see what was going on outside. It was just a matter of what you get used to, I supposed. Sitting up front with an unobstructed view of everything might have unnerved him.

It was about an hour before Bill unsnapped his oxygen mask and leaned over to shout, "The pilot says they need you up front." I nodded and unplugged my oxygen outlet, reattaching it to the walk-around bottle. I tiptoed along the catwalk through the bomb bay and dropped through the hatch into the nose. Damn, it was bright up here! I leaned forward in my seat and drank in the view as a man dying of thirst would gulp a glass of water.

They shot us up good at Cologne. The flak was heavy and it was accurate. I didn't see any of our planes go down, but they were getting bounced around by close bursts, and so were we. I went through the usual cycle of emotions—anxiety, fear, excitement, and finally relief. We came off the target with all four engines running and the Group strung out and scattered. Four P-51s slid back and forth around us like sheepdogs getting the flock back together after the wolves had panicked them.

I looked at my watch from time to time and finally decided I'd better get back to the dungeon. As near as I could tell I had used the walk-around bottle for about half-an-hour, and it was supposed to be a forty-five minute supply. I got on the intercom and told the pilot I was going to have to leave my position, and he gave me a "Roger." I took one last look around to be sure everything was the way it was supposed to be and trekked back to the radio room.

The trip back wasn't so bad. Bill was still busy with his monitoring chores, and I sat down and tried to keep from being bored. I rehashed my trip to London and wondered when I'd get back again. I wondered if Barbara would be able to get away next time or if she'd want to. My fantasizing was suddenly interrupted by the realization that I was cold as ice. The heated suit was just a thin nylon, with no warmth unless it was plugged into an electrical source.

I gazed at Bill's suit cord and followed it with my eyes along the floor, where it mixed in with other wires and paraphernalia. It terminated in a male/female jack plug behind his seat. I pretended to change my position on the floor, at the same time unplugging his cord and inserting mine in the jack. It took about ten or fifteen minutes before I felt the warmth of my suit. It took Bill almost an hour before he realized he was freezing. I saw him stop fooling with the dials and put down his pencil. Then he took off his gloves and rubbed his hands together, like you do when they're cold. He reached down to be sure his suit cord was OK, and pulled the cord until he came to the male plug. He swung around in his seat then and saw my plug. He yanked it out and threw it at me, then reattached his suit cord. He shook a fist at me and went back to what he was doing before the cold spell set it. I was warm as toast now and laughing like hell at how long it took him to realize he was freezing.

I could tell we were letting down but I had no altimeter. I unfastened my oxygen mask and let it hang to the side, and had no trouble breathing, so I put the mask back on, plugged into the bottle and went back up front. We were under 15,000 when I got back to my seat in the nose. I lit a cigarette, having a little trouble keeping the Zippo going long enough to light it. It felt good to be back home. When our tires squealed on the Podington runway I was leaning forward, as always, watching the left gear when the tire smoked and started to spin.

While we gathered our stuff together, taxiing around the perimeter strip, Jack asked me, "You going to put in for a Purple Heart?"

I said, "You don't know how close I came to making that a posthumous Purple Heart!"

The last two weeks of October dragged by in a series of stand-downs, Alerts, then more stand-downs, then another Alert, and always the rain. I just couldn't seem to get on the right list. On the couple of times I was alerted the missions were scrubbed, and the few times the Group got in the air I wasn't alerted. Finally, on October 30 I sat once again in the briefing room and saw the curtains drawn—and wished I wasn't there. The entire First and Third Divisions, almost a thousand B-17s, were going to Merseburg. And half that many B-24s from the Second Divison were bound for Hamburg. The oil refineries were going to get a shellacking today, I thought, and so were we.

But the weather changed our plans. Halfway to the target we got a recall. The weather had deteriorated so badly that it was impossible to get a shot at Merseburg, so we went looking for our Secondary. We found it, not visually but via PFF. And once again we tore up the railroad tracks in Münster.

There was only meager flak over the target. I figured it was because the Germans had tracked us toward Merseburg and didn't figure on our reversing direction and hitting Münster. The marshaling yards in Münster must have been knocked completely out of commission; we had put more than 450 *tons* on them. The Third Division, for some reason, had abandoned the mission and came back to England. But we got credit for another one, and when I logged it I didn't indicate "milk run" in my book. For some reason I thought it might be bad luck.

Late in October we got news about Charlie Hodges getting the Distinguished Service Cross. Charlie's name and his incredible exploit were well known to everybody in the Ninety-second, and especially to us in the 326th. His adventure happened on June 18, the day before I flew my very first mission. His saga had been recounted many times in the club and the mess and the local pub. I felt like I knew him well, although I had never met him. I was surprised, and disappointed, when I learned that he hadn't gotten the Congressional Medal of Honor. That's what he was recommended for, I had heard, and I couldn't understand why he wound up with only the second highest award for bravery.

Back in June, Charlie was leading the Group to Hamburg after the lead plane lost its radar over Helgoland. Just after bombs-away, banking to the right to get out of the flak, a shell exploded in the cockpit. The copilot's face was blown off and his body slumped forward over the control column. The plane went into a shallow dive.

Charlie's left leg had been blown off between the knee and the ankle, he was hit in the right knee and the jaw. The instrument panel had disappeared, blown completely away. Still in the middle of the flak, Charlie didn't know which way to go. But he knew it was time to turn on the tip tanks because the last time he'd seen the fuel gauge the main tanks were about empty.

The bombardier came up to see what had happened on the flight deck and Charlie yelled at him to turn on the tanks. Then he told him to go down and find out from the navigator which way to go to get back to England. In a minute the bombardier came back and pointed, "Go that-a-way!" Charlie aimed the B-17 in the direction the bombardier was pointing.

A crewman who knew something about flying but had never landed an airplane took over the controls so they could get Charlie down into the nose compartment and look after his wounds. His left leg was completely severed, but the stump had swelled from the traumatic amputation and he wasn't losing much blood. The bombardier and navigator put sulfanilamide on his wounds and gave him a shot of morphine. All the while Charlie was giving orders and directing the whole operation. Somebody said, "We're going to try to fly to Sweden."

Charlie said, "The hell you are! You're flying to England!"

And that was what they did. With the navigator sending instructions to the novice at the controls, who had no instruments but just tried to aim where the bombardier pointed, they flew 650 miles across the North Sea and crossed the English coast at the *exact spot* they had left it more than six hours before!

Charlie Hodges' B-17 came over the field flying sideways and almost hit the control tower before the novice pilot got it straightened out. He finally lined it up with the main runway and got it on the ground. Charlie yelled, "That was a beautiful landing!"

During this entire ordeal there was never any doubt about who was in charge. Charlie gave orders, he monitored his own blood loss using his wrist watch, and at one point said, "Hell, I can fly better than that with one leg. Get me back up there!"

Charlie Hodges was a cocky twenty-two years old when he went home to a wife, a newborn son, and an artificial leg. And the nation's second-highest award for bravery.

Two days after Charlie's exploit over Hamburg I was over that same place, scared half to death. Now, five months later, I was still flying, unscathed except for having been knocked silly by an oxygen regulator.

Combat flying was mostly luck. Maybe it was all luck.

FIFTEEN

NO PLACE TO HIDE

The end of one month and the beginning of another held no particular significance to me. It was just a way of keeping track of time. A month ago I had started with a degree of optimism about finishing my tour by the first of November. Now it *was* the first of November and I was only two missions closer to finishing than I had been on the last day of September. It had rained twenty-three days out of thirty-one in October. So I made no predictions, not even to myself, about November. Whatever happened would happen.

A Maximum Effort Alert went up on the first day of the month and I was on the list. Morning came early. By four-thirty I was sitting in a briefing room that was filled to capacity. There was a kind of electricity in the air, a feeling that this was going to be a "big show," as the British might say. We even had a guest this morning, a member of the press. Herb Palmer, a combat reporter from *Stars and Stripes*, was introduced. And this until-now non-combatant second lieutenant, who had been on the base for a week or more gathering information for a story, was going with us on the mission—to Merseburg. I wondered if that name meant anything to him; it did to me, and to everybody else in the room, and he must have heard the moans and the muttered protests when the curtain was pulled back.

My squadron, the 326th, was leading the First Air Division today. Major "Moose" Hardin, our squadron C.O., was piloting the lead plane and Colonel Wilson was flying copilot and was air division commander. Erro Michaelson, our cool-nerved, deadeye bombardier, was naturally the man selected to put the bombs where they were supposed to go. Our visiting correspondent Herb Palmer was flying as waist gunner on the lead plane. If he was expecting this to be a typical combat mission, he was in for a surprise. If Merseburg lived up to its reputation, he might better carry an extra pair of shorts!

I left the briefing room with the feeling that this was as big an event as D-Day. In the equipment room I heard somebody say, "Night before last I was bobbing for apples at the Halloween party, and today I'm going to play trick or treat over Merseburg!" The American G.I. had an uncanny knack for summing up a situation with a sardonic ad-lib.

Today I didn't stare at the black cloud over Merseburg, while dreading the moment we would turn into it. There *was* no black cloud, just blue sky. We were the first to arrive, and we'd test the water for the six groups that would follow us through. They could watch us and dread the time it would be their turn.

The flak didn't start with a few bursts, then build up to a box barrage. Instead it materialized with unbelievable speed, bursting everywhere at once. In a matter of seconds the sky was dirtied with black and I was scrunched up inside my flak suit, trying to be as small as possible. I had that same numb feeling that I had before, almost as if I was resigned to the fact that I was going to get killed in a few minutes. And there wasn't a damn thing I could do about it.

After bombs-away the flak didn't stop. The lead plane started a slow bank to the right and then took two, or maybe three flak bursts. He fell out of formation, and in a few seconds was somewhere below and behind us, out of my sight. Then we took a direct hit that sounded like it was inside the airplane. I tore at the fasteners on my flak suit and finally it fell to the floor. I grabbed the parachute pack on my right and slammed the D-rings into the harness snaps. I checked to be sure it wasn't on upside-down, and it looked terribly small. I expected to hear the order to bail out any second.

Everybody was on the intercom, calling out flak at something-o'clock, asking what the hell happened, until Shorty yelled "Get off the damn intercom!" and told the engineer to go down and check the damage. Number two engine had stopped and the prop was feathered. The flak had stopped and we were still flying with the rest of the squadron. I decided we weren't going to hit the silk today, but I didn't take off the parachute pack.

In a few minutes Shorty's voice snapped over the intercom. He gave us a damage report. We had taken a hit right under the flight deck and it had made a mess of everything down there, but nothing that would keep us from flying. He called for a crew check, and the confusion and chaos disappeared, replaced by the disciplined responses: "Tail gunner OK—Waist OK—Ball turret OK—"

We had escaped from Merseburg again, still in one piece. The airplane wasn't in such great shape but the nine men inside it didn't suffer so much as a cut finger. After awhile it became just another long ride back to England. Somebody asked, "Did you see the lead plane go down? He looked like he'd had it!" I felt a twinge of guilt about my amusement this morning when I anticipated Herb Palmer's introduction to combat flying. The poor bastard might be dead by now. They might all be dead by now.

The ride back to Podington was uneventful. The landing wasn't. I was leaning forward in the nose, as usual, and Shorty greased it in with that fighter-pilot style of his. I was still watching the left main gear when I realized we weren't slowing down like we should be. I straightened up in my seat and was about to glance over at my airspeed indicator when I saw Jack's butt going through the hatch under the flight deck. I jerked my head around and looked out the nose and saw the end of the runway coming up, fast! Goddamit, we've got no brakes!

By the time everything had registered in my brain and I turned around to get out of the nose we were off the end of the runway. We hit a ditch with such impact that I went forward into the Plexiglas at the same time Jack's left cheek-gun swung forward on its bungee cord and whammed me in the back. By now we were well out into a wheat field and slowing down, so I just lay there and looked ahead to see if there were any obstructions in front of us. There was a little line of trees ahead, at the opposite edge of the field, but we were slowed down so much that they weren't a problem. We rolled to a bumpy stop and I didn't waste any time opening the nose hatch and dropping to the ground. I noticed it didn't seem very far from the hatch to the ground.

In a couple of minutes we were all out of the wrecked plane and the ambulance and fire truck were bumping across the wheat field toward us. Shorty casually asked if everybody was OK. All of us were. "Is that airplane sitting too low, or is it just the wheat that makes it look like that?" I asked.

"I tried to pull up the gear before we went off the runway, but it only came partway up," Shorty replied.

What happened was simple, and probably saved my hide. When the main gear started to come up, the weight of the airplane bent the struts and they locked up, preventing the gear from fully retracting. If it had retracted all the way, the chin turret would have jammed into the ground and pushed up into the nose compartment, with me sitting on top of it. I pointed this out to Shorty, and he grinned and said, "You shouldn't stay in the nose for landings."

Our B-17 was totaled. Not only was it full of holes, but the impact of hitting the ditch had bent the fuselage and there were big wrinkles in the skin just back of the radio room. It would be scrapped for parts. It was fifteen minutes or so before a truck got there to take us back to the base. We stood there looking at our crippled B-17, walking around it and commenting on the holes, jagged tears in the aluminum. Although we didn't say it, I know we were all thinking the same thing: how did we manage to destroy an airplane and not a single one of us get hurt?

We all assumed that we had lost one today, Moose Hardin's plane. But when we got to Interrogation we found out that they were down on the English coast and at least some of them were OK. It took a while, but bit by bit we learned what had happened to *Satan's Lady* after it was blown out of the sky over Merseburg. The flak bursts that caught the lead plane knocked out two engines and injured six of the crew. They continued to lose altitude even after jettisoning everything except the machine guns and ammo. Hardin got the airplane more or less under control and, since there were some 400 German fighters in the area, he decided to fly just above the cloud deck at 7,000 feet, so that he could dive into the clouds if the Messerschmitts showed up. If they spotted a crippled airplane, they would sure as hell be there.

Hardin and Colonel Wilson nursed the B-17 along and were almost at the Dutch border when ice on the wings sent them into a flat spin to the right. They manhandled the big plane out of the spin, and immediately went into a spin to the left. During the last spin, Hardin ordered a bailout. Three men jumped—Captain Hall and Lieutenant Knoble, the co-navigators, and Lieutenant John Staples, who was flying as tail gunner, but was actually Moose Hardin's regular copilot.

Hardin finally got the B-17 under control again and rescinded the bailout order. They were down to less than 5,000 feet when they approached the English Channel. At this point they threw the machine guns and ammo overboard to try to lighten the airplane. Moose headed for the emergency strip on the coast, RAF Station Woodbridge. He circled for a landing and found that the landing gear and flap controls had been shot out, so he just gently floated the plane in on its belly. The flying control officer at Woodbridge said it was the best crash-landing he'd ever seen.

The waist gunner was Bob, the guy who bunked next to me, and I got a good bit of information from him about what had actually happened. One of the things he said was that he thought Staples had bailed out without his parachute. Apparently they found a parachute pack in the back of the plane after the crash-landing. Happily this turned out to be an extra parachute, so Staples was assumed to be alive, if not necessarily well, somewhere in Germany.

The trip to Merseburg cost the First Division dearly. Two-hundred-ten B-17s flew over the target and twenty-six were shot down. These didn't include airplanes like Moose's and ours, that got back to England or France, but only those that were destroyed in combat. The German staff sergeant gunners at Merseburg hit all but thirty-one airplanes. I was surprised that they missed any.

So I had gone back to Merseburg again and survived. But Merseburg remained solidly entrenched in its position as Number One on the Target Priority List and was scheduled to receive attention on a more regular basis. About ten percent of all the synthetic fuel in Germany was produced there, we were told, and we could expect to be visiting the place on a regular basis. I felt sure that the Germans were at this very moment bringing in more flak guns, and more staff sergeants to man them. I logged Merseburg as my twenty-ninth mission and added a brief four-word description: "WORST I EVER SAW!" Then after a moment's reflection I underlined the words.

After a stand-down on the third to give the ground crews a chance to repair the damage we took at Merseburg, we went out after German oil again on the fourth. Hamburg, actually a suburb of Harburg, was probably second to Merseburg in the production of synthetic fuel, and it hadn't been hit for awhile, at least not by us.

The mission turned out to be an absolute milk run and I couldn't figure out why. We bombed PFF, but that was nothing new, and the German gunners could shoot just as well through cloud cover as they could visually, or so it would seem. But today there was very little flak, and what there was didn't seem to be at all accurate. Happily I logged the easy mission and just as happily added another Oak Leaf Cluster to my Air Medal ribbon. November was shaping up much differently than October.

I flew again the next day. I hadn't done two in a row since August. We gave the oil refineries a rest and tore up the railroad yard at Frankfurt. It was the first time we had bombed visually in a while. The sky was partly clear over Germany and the Eighth was out in force. More than 1,200 B-17s and B-24s pounded targets all over the Third Reich.

I logged Frankfurt as a milk run, then added "(With flak)" in parentheses. Either my cockiness was returning or, as seemed more likely, I was exhilarated to be getting so close to the end of my tour.

The Group went back to Hamburg on November 6 but I wasn't alerted for that one, and on the seventh there was a stand-down. I was rested and ready to go, and made the list for the eighth. When I saw the target map I wished I'd gone on sick call. We were going back to Merseburg. There was no joy in the briefing room that morning.

I got off the truck and lugged my gear across the pitch-dark hardstand. I could barely make out the outline of the B-17. I must be the first one here, I thought. I opened the nose hatch and shoved my gear into the compartment. I wasn't exactly depressed, but I wasn't in the best spirits either. There really wasn't much to cheer me up. It was cold, damp, dark, and I was going back to a target that scared the pants off me. I decided to go ahead and pre-flight the nose compartment, and grabbed the top of the hatch. I swung my feet through the opening and started to wriggle through. At this point all hell broke loose.

A burst of machine-gun fire that sounded like it was right under me broke the absolute quiet of the morning. The B-17 shook like it had come alive. I went limp as a dishrag and dropped to the concrete like a stone. I landed on my tailbone and it hurt like hell, but I was too numb with shock to wonder if I had broken anything. I just laid there, and my brain still hadn't started trying to figure out what had happened.

I may have yelled when I fell; I have no idea whether I did or not. But in a few seconds I saw a shadowy form coming toward me from under the fuselage. He was bent over in a crouch and I didn't recognize him until he asked if I was OK. It was Koehne, the ball turret gunner. I didn't answer him about being OK or not, but asked, "What the hell happened?" Koehne helped me get to my feet and said, "Oh, shit, I really screwed up!"

By the time we got to the mechanics' tent a jeep screeched to a stop on the hardstand and an officer jumped out. He was wearing an armband and I guess he was the O.D. He wanted to know what the hell was going on, and I let Koehne explain it. I didn't know myself what had happened, but my mind was beginning to put the pieces together.

Koehne was sitting under the airplane behind his ball turret, installing his machine guns. After he got everything in place he checked the firing solenoids, which was S.O.P. Just push the plunger in with a pencil and if you hear a double click, you know it's working. The only thing he did out of sequence was to hand-charge the gun *before* he checked the solenoid. The gun worked fine. A half a dozen caliber-fifty slugs went ricocheting through the woods.

It was impossible to describe the shattering sound a caliber-fifty makes in the stillness of an English morning. My nerves were shot, my butt was sore, and I still had to go to Merseburg. This day was not starting out right at all.

Merseburg was different, for me, than any other target. The queasy stomach and the feeling of dread never let up, from the time I saw the target string at briefing until we were well away from the area. The bomb run itself was somehow different there. There was more going on, more activity on the intercom. The staccato of excited voices— "Flak at four o'clock!"—"Damn, that one was close!"—"See any of our escort fighters?"—continued until finally the pilot told us not to use the damn intercom unless it was an emergency. Merseburg seemed to bring out the baser instincts in all of us, mainly fear.

I didn't know it until it was all over, but I came very close to getting my head shot off that day. The pop of close bursts and the sound of flak hitting our airplane were very distinct, but I couldn't tell where we were being hit. It was always somewhere behind me. After all, there wasn't anything to hit in front of me but a thin sheet of Plexiglas.

The pilot's voice on the intercom finally caught my attention. It was the second time he'd asked if we were OK in the nose. The bombs were gone and the doors were closed and I was turning off switches and looking around anxiously to see how much flak was still with us. The second time I heard the query about our well-being I responded, after glancing over my shoulder to be sure Jack was still in his flak suit foxhole.

"Yeah, we're OK down here. Any problem?"

"Look up over your head!"

Just above and slightly behind the nose of a B-17, mounted in the ceiling of the compartment, is a little Plexiglas dome. It was called the "astrodome," about a foot and a half in diameter and nine or ten inches high. It was there for the navigator to use if he needed to take readings with his sextant. I turned around in my seat and looked up. Our astrodome wasn't there any more. It was gone, blown completely away, with just a couple of jagged pieces of Plexiglas jutting out of the rim. Jack looked up at the ragged hole, then we looked at each other. We were both wondering the same thing. Which way was the flak going when it tore out our ceiling? We made an inspection of the compartment, but couldn't find any more holes that weren't supposed to be there, so we shrugged and helped one another get out of the flak suits.

Psychologically Merseburg was the same as before, but statistically it wasn't all that bad this time. We didn't lose any airplanes, and the Division lost only three out of 200. About eighty-five planes were damaged, a much lower percentage than the staff sergeant gunners usually hit.

During the trip home I had to use the relief tube and I forgot to call the ball turret gunner and warn him to turn his guns to the rear. It was unintentional; Merseburg just had me shook up. But I'm sure Koehne thought I did it on purpose, just to get even for that morning. His voice came through on the intercom loud, clear, and *mad*: "Sonofabitch, who did that?"

"Who did what?" somebody else's voice asked.

"Pissed on my turret, that's what! I can't see a damn thing!"

I kept very quiet. I hadn't intended to do it. I always warned him in advance. But I was just slightly amused at having coated his windows with a layer of opaque yellow ice.

The day after Merseburg I was sitting in the briefing room, not nearly so early as the previous day, listening to one of those fascinating explanations of where we were going, and why, and what we were going to do when we got there. The day's mission promised to be interesting, important, and a milk run in the bargain.

General Patton's fast-moving Third Army had almost reached the

German border, but was stopped cold at Metz. Patton's tanks had encircled the ancient city in northern France, but Metz was a fortress. It had been since the middle ages, only now it was filled with Germans and very heavy artillery. The Aisne Forts overlooked the city, and the German guns were pointed right down old Blood-and-Guts's throat. Low-level attacks by fighter-bombers didn't have the punch to knock out the heavy fortifications. Patton needed some heavy tonnage to get rid of this obstacle, the kind of tonnage that the Eighth Air Force could deliver.

The only problem was the weather. Metz was covered by ten-tenths cloud, so we'd have to go in via PFF. To me that always seemed risky, when our own troops were close to the target. At bombardiers' briefing we studied target maps and photos, although there wasn't a chance we'd be able to see the ground. The last words were, "Don't toggle early and don't toggle late. Keep your heads out of your asses and watch what's going on!"

The actual mission wasn't as interesting as the briefing. We went in straight and level and tight and dropped at the same instant, almost as if the bombs all came from the same B-17. Then we came home. I hoped we made General Patton happy. It sure as hell made me happy. Now I had only two to go!

The mission turned out to be a total success. General Doolittle, always quick to praise when he thought it was due, forwarded his commendation, along with thanks from the commanding general of the British XX Corps. If Patton said anything it wasn't passed on to us; I guessed he just didn't take the time. From what I'd heard of him, he probably had the tanks moving before we were out of the target area.

I had flown four missions in a week, and prayed that the momentum would continue. It didn't. We went on stand-down, and it sounded like it would be for an extended period. Damn this weather! Just a couple of decent flying days, that was all I needed.

After three days of trying to find something to do with my time, I decided I might as well be in London, since there wasn't going to be any flying done for now. Jack Fromkin agreed to come along with me.

While I was in the squadron office the exec approached me and mentioned that he had just discovered that I hadn't had my two weeks at the flak house. Every flyer was entitled to this R&R and usually took it about midway through a tour. I told the exec that I had, very frankly, forgotten about this and that at this late date I really didn't want to cool my heels at some manor house for two weeks. I only had two missions to go, and I knew that the longer I put them off, the more my anxiety was going to build up. I didn't say that to the exec, of course; I didn't have to. He knew the feeling.

"It's certainly not mandatory," he said, "but you're entitled to go if you want to."

"Sir, I think a few days in London would do me as much good as the flak house," I replied.

Jack and I checked in at the Winston and got a room one flight up. The room was tiny but had two beds and Jack was impressed with my having an "inside track" at this neat little hotel, tucked away just off Piccadilly. I had phoned the night before and left word for Barbara but there was no message at the desk when I checked in. I decided to call the number she'd given me for her home, and got her dad on the line. He sounded very cordial, and seemed to know all about me.

"I'm afraid Barbara's got some sort of extra duty, but she said she'd perhaps be free tomorrow afternoon."

I didn't know quite what to say, and finally said, "Oh, I see."

He chuckled and said, "Tough luck, old chap!"

Jack and I had a pleasant afternoon. We hit most of the familiar bars and pubs, occasionally interrupted by sightseeing walks around the city. We found ourselves in the Universelle Brasserie, which he wasn't familiar with. We wound up drinking with two Canadian tank officers and after a couple of hours one of them suggested we leave the place, since there didn't seem to be any unattached girls. He had a membership card in a private club that he said was a great place . . . plenty of girls, dancing, a pretty good orchestra. Jack and I were all for it and the four of us left the table and made our way through the shoulder to shoulder people and up the stairs. We were still trying to get our eyes oriented to the darkness when I discovered I'd left my billfold in the Brasserie. My beautiful English wallet with the watered-silk lining was stuffed with pound notes and "fivers"—about 200 bucks' worth!

I was determined to go back and look for it, but I had a sick feeling that I had seen the last of it. So had Jack and the two Canucks.

"Somebody probably picked your pocket. Hell, you'll never find it."

"No, I know damn well nobody lifted it. It was in my inside pocket. I just left it on the table, I'm sure of it."

"Well, it's gone by now."

Jack said he'd lend me some money, but I was determined to go back and check. Finally, Jack said he'd go back with me to check and we'd meet them at this so-called private club later.

We walked downstairs and back into the sea of people and the cloud of cigarette smoke. We finally found the table where we'd been sitting. It was occupied by three civilians now, and the table was littered with paper napkins, beer glasses, and ash trays. I said, "Pardon me, but we were just sitting here and I think I left something. OK if I check?"

With typical British courtesy they smiled and one of them waved his hand over the table and said, "Righto, Yank, 'ave a look."

I picked up a pile of dirty napkins and there was my wallet. The English guys' eyes bulged a little, and I opened the wallet and sort of flipped through the money inside. It hadn't been touched.

I smiled and said, "Thanks a lot, gentlemen. Good night."

They looked at one another in disbelief as Jack and I headed back through the crowd. Jack shook his head and said, "Koger, you are one lucky bastard. The odds against that happening have got to be a million to one!"

Jack and I never made it to our friend's club. We tried for a while to get a cab, but couldn't find one that wasn't occupied. I had heard that the Piccadilly Commandos frequently hired cabs for the evening and used them as mobile whorehouses: a "quickie in the taxi for ten shillings" or a pound or whatever. Whether that's true or not I couldn't say, but hiring a taxi after dark was next to impossible.

We went to the Windmill Theater and caught most of the last show. It was stripteasers and comics and song and dance, bawdy and loud with spotlights moving here and there constantly to focus briefly on almost nude gals. The English strippers weren't nearly as athletic as their American counterparts. Just before coming to England I had caught the show at the famous "Old Howard" in Boston. The featured stripper was Sally the Tassel Dancer, and she did things with her body that I didn't know could be done. The English girls were better looking, and didn't go in for the bumps and grinds. They just removed their clothes in a very seductive manner and posed.

It was probably two in the morning when we got back to the Winston. We'd both had too much to drink, but Jack was really stoned. When he was drunk he shuffled along like a sleepwalker and I don't think he could really see where he was going. We walked up the stairs to our floor. I stayed behind Jack to catch him if he fell. When we got to the top he muttered, "Which way?" and I said, "To the right." He walked down the hall and I stopped momentarily, groping through my pockets for the room key. When I looked up Jack was opening the door to the elevator and was about to step into an empty shaft. I don't know how he got it opened, but somehow he did, and there was no elevator there to step into. I grabbed him by the shoulder and closed the gate. I said, "Damn, Fromkin, you just about jumped down an elevator shaft!"

"Oh?" he said.

I called Dulwich the next morning and spoke with a corporal who said Barbara couldn't come to the phone, but I got the idea she was not on duty that afternoon. Jack and I sat in the l'Auberge having coffee and talking about things to do. He didn't really care about charging out and walking around London or taking tours; he seemed content to loaf around the hotel and relax. So I decided that instead of waiting for a message from Barbara I'd go out to Dulwich. It was a half-hour train ride and I had nothing better to do anyway.

I walked down Grange Lane, alongside the stone wall that seemed to go on forever. At night it had seemed very romantic, an old garden wall in the moonlight. Today it was just a wall around an artillery installation. About fifty yards along the lane there was an opening in the wall with an iron gate that was swung partially open. I decided this would be a handy shortcut and walked in. I could see some military-looking buildings over to the left and about 200 yards ahead, so I cut across toward them. The area I was in was filled with little miniature Quonset huts, and they seemed to be full of artillery shells and rockets. I stopped to look inside one of the huts and examine the rockets. They were about five feet long and maybe six-inches in diameter, and I was wondering how they were used when a loud female voice literally brought me to attention. "You there! What are you doing here?"

I looked around. A slender British officer, female-type, was approaching. She had three pips on each shoulder—a Major—and clutched a swagger stick which was tucked under her right arm. She walked with authority, and she talked with authority. "How did you get in here, and why?"

I saluted and stammered, "Through the gate over there, ma'am."

She looked over at the wall and asked, "You mean it was open?"

"Yes ma'am."

"What is your business here?"

"I came to see Barbara Hardin. She's in 427 Battery."

"Have you been here before?"

"Just once. Not on the base, actually. I just walked with Barbara from the station to the gate."

The Major suddenly changed completely, from a martinet-type British officer to a very pleasant lady. She astonished me by inviting me to "come along and we can have a cup of tea while we locate your friend." We walked along a pathway to a building and walked inside an orderly room. The Major asked a girl in uniform to see about locating Private Hardin and then led the way into a sort of day room. There were three or four uniformed girls there, relaxing or reading, and they stood up when we came in. The Major and I sat down and talked for a few minutes. She asked me several questions, almost like a mother quizzing her daughter's beau, but she seemed to like me. After a while she excused herself and left.

I was right at home when Barbara walked in. Chatting with the girls gave me a chance to look over the selection in case Barbara was on duty. Barbara was free to sign out, so about two-thirty we walked to the station and waited for the London train. She seemed very happy to see me, and I think she was flattered that I went to so much effort to find her. I asked her what she'd like to do, and she said she didn't care, so I suggested dinner and a movie.

London was fun, as always, but much more so with Barbara tagging along. We talked about everything, but nothing serious except the fact that the buzz-bomb blitz was apparently over. Allied troops had now captured the last of the launching sites, it was believed. After dinner we went to the Odeon where an American technicolor movie called "Home in Indiana" was playing.

At some point during the movie I found myself thinking about my last two missions, and I realized my hands were trembling. The more I thought about it the worse it became, and I actually started to sweat. I had a terrible sense of foreboding, and I couldn't account for it. I tried to get it out of my mind, but I just couldn't concentrate on the movie. Barbara noticed that something was wrong and asked if I felt all right. I said, "Yes, I've just got the jitters. What do you say we get out of here and go someplace else?"

After we left the movie we walked along the dark sidewalk, going nowhere in particular. I confessed to her that I'd had an attack of nerves, for some reason I couldn't understand. Jokingly I said, "I suppose I'm getting flak-happy."

She thought this was nonsense and that it was only natural that I should be apprehensive, being so close to the end of my tour. We wandered into a bar called the Salted Almond. It was in a hotel, a very elegant one, I think, because the bar was beautiful. It had cozy little booths, dim lighting, and ornate, cut-glass mirrors on the walls. The bartender was a black man in a red velvet jacket, and he spoke with an upper-class English accent.

We sat in a little booth just across from the end of the bar and talked and drank for probably two hours. I did most of the drinking, and a good bit of the talking. Barbara was a good listener and had a pleasantly optimistic attitude. After a while I felt fine again, except for being a little bewildered about why I had gotten the shakes. I wasn't embarrassed about it, certainly not with Barbara; I just couldn't understand what caused it. It was a terrible feeling of depression, of impending doom. I hoped to hell it didn't happen again. Surely to God, I thought, I'm not going to get killed at this late date!

I insisted on riding the train back to Dulwich with Barbara. She in turn insisted it wasn't necessary, but I had other plans. My intention was to bushwhack her. I had tried to put the make on her from the time we met, with no success. But now I had gotten to know her better and I thought maybe under the right circumstances she would give in.

My plan was very simple: just before train time I told her I was going to dash over to the kiosk and see if they had any chocolates. She said hurry, we'd miss the train, but I assured her it would only be a minute. I walked back and said they were out of chocolates and we walked down the platform. She started to get into a coach, but I said let's try farther on. Finally I spotted a compartment that was empty and said, "Here, let's take this one." The train pulled out of the station and we were alone in the compartment. She couldn't escape unless she jumped off a moving train!

It didn't work, though I tried mightily. She knew exactly what I was planning and was mildly amused at it, but she just wasn't that kind of girl. She didn't put it in those words. She didn't have to.

We walked down Grange Lane, along the endless wall, and I wasn't at all angry or upset at her. I consoled myself with the thought that a half-hour train trip just wasn't enough time, although I doubted that I could have talked her into it if we had gone all the way to Scotland.

We said good night at the main gate and she said next time she saw me I'd probably be all done with combat flying. I promised to call and walked back down Grange Lane toward the station, pondering my preference in girlfriends. I always seemed to pick the "nice girl" type, and wondered if I wouldn't have just as much fun with the ones with dyed hair and too much makeup and short tight dresses and round heels. Probably not, I thought.

My thoughts drifted back to my last two missions, but not with the terrible feeling I'd had sitting in the Odeon. When I realized how many thirty-three were and how few *two* were by comparison, I felt a sense of anticipation rather than apprehension. Hell, I was almost finished!

SIXTEEN

NO PLACE TO LAND

The weather was not just bad, it was horrible. The Ninety-second was ground-bound. Not only in England but on the Continent the clouds and the rain and the fog persisted. Of course we could bomb through overcast, but bombing requires takeoffs and landings. Nobody in his right mind would even think about filling the English sky with B-17s to mill around blindly in the thick gray blanket, unless he wanted to set a new record for midair collisions. Then there was the even more impossible problem of getting them back on the ground.

Finally somebody at High Wycombe decided we *had* to get off the ground. The order came down on the fifteenth for a mission. We bitched and moaned about having to get up at three in the morning and go through all the motions when there wasn't a chance in hell of actually taking off.

Briefing on the sixteenth was another battle situation report. Our troops had just captured their first German city, Aachen. It was barely in Germany, only about four miles from the Belgian border, but it *was* in Germany. And it was in American hands, even though the issue, from what I could gather from the G-2 briefing officer, was still somewhat in doubt. Our troops were moving northeast toward Cologne, but just outside Aachen had run into stiff and stubborn resistance from the Germans. They were apparently equipped with Panzers, infantry, and artillery, and intended not only to stop our advance but to retake Aachen. So once again the Mighty Eighth was called on to put a few hundred tons where it would do the most good. This would be the Eschweiler area, just a few miles northeast of Aachen. That's where most of the Germans were.

We spent a long time in bombardiers' briefing studying aerial photos marked with the last known locations of enemy and friendly troops and familiarizing ourselves with an area that we wouldn't be able to see from the air. The German heavy guns were in fixed locations but the troops and Panzers could well be repositioned by now. The bomb line meandered along well in front of our farthest advanced U.S. troops. But the bomb line was imaginary, and everything else would be underneath a solid ten-tenths cloud cover. So it was another case of "Don't drop late and for damn sure don't drop early. Stay alert and don't get hypnotized watching the lead plane. Our own guys are down there!"

I walked out into the wet, foggy chill and headed for the equipment room with the other bombardiers. Somebody said, "All this shit and this thing will be scrubbed for sure!" Somebody else said, "I'm not so sure. Sounds like we're starting a major offensive and this is a must-go situation." I said, "Guys, it's my next to last one and I hope to hell we get off the ground!"

If we did get off this would be a real milk run, I thought. G-2 had predicted little or no enemy resistance, barring the unlikely possibility that a bunch of German fighters decided to chew us up. "Unlikely" was my interpretation, not G-2's; those guys had fighters on the brain. They warned us constantly that the Luftwaffe was not dead.

Takeoff and landing were all I was concerned about. We had made takeoffs in this kind of stuff before. I tried to recall what the weather officer had said about base conditions for our return, but couldn't remember. Oh well, I thought, they sure as hell wouldn't have sent us out if there was no place to land when we got back.

But that's *exactly* what they did.

We roared down the dark, foggy runway and I couldn't even see the edges. I decided that the pilot must be just watching the compass. After we lifted off we spent a long time in the thick, gray overcast. I kept my nose almost against the Plexiglas trying to watch for other B-17s, even though I knew that if I saw one it would probably be just before we collided. Then we broke through into the bright blue morning sky and the tenseness went out of my body in a sudden surge.

We drifted lazily around above the cloud deck, forming up the Group and climbing to altitude. I knew when we crossed the English coastline only because the navigator said we had; I couldn't see it. I went back and pulled the arming pins. We were loaded with 500-pound bundles of fragmentation bombs, banded together with steel strapping.

The bomb run was straight and smooth and free of any distraction. The flak-free sky was suddenly filled with hundreds of bombs, tumbling and wobbling as they separated from their companions. I could see the steel strapping falling among the bombs as they finally responded to their fins and started on their trajectory toward the white mass of clouds. In a few seconds they had disappeared into the clouds and we flew straight on, almost as if turning away might in some way influence the point of impact of the bombs we had just dropped. I closed the doors, went through the routine of acknowledgments from the radioman, and happily called for an oxygen check. We should be back on the ground in a couple of hours.

It didn't turn out to be that easy. Halfway across the channel we were notified that all the airfields in the Midlands and East Anglia were completely socked in. We could either try to find an open airfield somewhere in the west of England, or else go back to France and see if we could find one there. The third alternative was to ditch our damn airplanes in the Channel, but apparently that wasn't suggested.

We headed for the west of England. I could see only solid clouds below us and had no idea where we were. Jack was busy with his little G-box, watching the blips on the scope and looking somewhat concerned; I didn't think he knew where we were, either. I hoped to hell somebody did.

After flying for about an hour, changing course frequently as if we were searching blindly for some place without clouds, I got the impression that we were getting ready to land. The pilot had lowered the flaps partway, and finally the main gear swung down and locked. I peered at the ground, but still couldn't see any. The clouds were thinner, I could tell that much, but there was no place open enough to land a B-17 that I could see. I assumed the pilot was on the radio talking to the group lead, and that *he* was talking to somebody on the ground who knew where there was a place we could land. I was beginning to get really worried when we peeled off and swung into our approach to a runway that I now could barely make out. It was raining hard. The water was running from the point of the Plexiglas nose in little rivers back along the nosecone to the fuselage.

As we got closer I could make out the runway and then spotted some airplanes parked here and there around it. They were bombers, it looked like, but not B-17s or B-24s. We finally touched down with a couple of little bounces—I figured Shorty might be a little nervous by now, along with the rest of us—and I could feel the brakes being applied in gentle little taps. The rain was really coming down and the airfield was covered with menacing-looking clouds that moved across it in rows, one after the other.

I was as relieved to be on the ground as I was when we came out of a flak barrage. We turned off the runway and taxied along a narrow strip that I assumed was a perimeter track. We passed a couple of hardstands and I saw the bombers up close. They were Wellingtons, with big RAF roundels on the fuselages. We taxied and stopped, taxied and stopped, turned and stopped, then taxied some more. It seemed to me that we had circled the airfield before we finally stopped and the engines wound down. The props slowed to a stop, and our milk run to Aachen was over. We weren't home, but we were safe on the ground once again.

We left our chutes and harnesses and other gear in the airplane and crawled out. Some RAF guys and W.A.A.F.'s pointed toward a building and we headed for it. We went inside and discovered a large ready room, much like our equipment room. The place was bedlam, with American flyers everywhere and RAF personnel being very polite in trying to sort things out. From what I had seen this wasn't a very large base, and unexpected houseguests in the form of 400 Americans was undoubtedly disconcerting.

Our haven in the storm turned out to be a little place called Barford St. John. Because it was a Wellington base, I assumed it was a combat group, but it was actually an O.T.U.—Operations Training Unit. We were going to be there for awhile, we found out. It was not just the weather; our airplanes were not in the best condition. Some were damaged, not so much from enemy action as the landing. In our haste to get our forty-eight B-17s on the ground, using one runway and limited taxi-ways, planes ended up mired three-feet deep in mud, some with bent props. Our landing had been a real circus.

The RAF traffic controller at Barford was, according to reports, a basket case. He was accustomed to the disciplined takeoffs and landings of the Wellingtons, who didn't all try to get off the ground or on it at one time. They took off at five-minute intervals, and returned the same way; the British night bombing involved a "bomber stream" rather than a tight formation.

Over the next day and a half I met quite a few RAF people and learned a lot about how they lived and worked. There were quite a number of Canadians at Barford, identifiable by the RCAF insignia on their wings. They seemed a little more happy-go-lucky than the British, and certainly more outspoken. One RCAF pilot I was talking with said, "The Brits have all the administrative jobs and the combat crews are all Canadians!" This was no doubt an exaggeration, but from several comments and from my own observations it seemed that there was a sort of separation along nationalistic lines.

Our hosts provided us with quarters as best they could, and we slept wherever there was space. Dinner was boiled potatoes and dark bread, and there were jars of peanut butter and orange marmalade on the tables, and big white mugs of hot tea.

I spent part of the evening with a cute W.A.A.F. corporal in crew supply room. She hadn't been around many Americans and was inquisitive. How did we feel about being here? What did I think about daylight bombing? How many "ops" had I done? She was also flirtatious, and teasingly pretended to protect the flying gloves and boots and helmets to be sure I didn't pinch anything. She knew very well that it wasn't her precious flying gear that I wanted to pinch.

The following day was spent in trying to get our planes out of the mud and in flying condition. We didn't really have much to do with that; several dozen ground crewmen from the Ninety-second had come over and had worked through the night and all the next day at this thankless task. The rain hadn't let up, either.

We got back to Podington on the eighteenth, wearing the same clothes we put on more than forty-eight hours before, and sporting two-day beards.

The stand-down continued until the twenty-first.

The Aachen raid was a mess from our point of view, but a total success from the military standpoint. General Doolittle sent a glowing commendation and passed along the comments of the general who commanded the infantry division for whom we paved the way with bombs:

On November 16 the Eighth Air Force performed one of its most outstanding operations. The force took off under extremely adverse base weather conditions and successfully attacked targets on the immediate front of our ground troops almost exclusively by instrument technique with very good results. Ground commanders were highly pleased and report all bombs on or near the targets, with no injuries to friendly troops. It was a difficult task well done and I commend you for the capable and efficient manner in which it was conducted.

It is a pleasure to forward the following message from the CG 104th Infantry Division: "Doughboys thank you for a fine job. Certainly appreciated it. Please inform all participants. Terry Allen." Such a message typifies the teamwork which is doing so much to knock out our common enemy. J. H. Doolittle.

Doughboys? I hadn't heard that term applied to ground-pounders except in books and movies about World War I. General Terry de la Mesa Allen had been in that one, too.

I got my D.F.C. before I finished my tour. I suppose that was customary. They figured I'd make the last two, and if I didn't I could have it posthumously. The ceremony was very military and, to me, very impressive. We wore Class-A uniforms again and Colonel Wilson appeared to be genuinely proud of us. He handed me the case along with a firm handshake and a warm smile, "Congratulations!"

I hadn't seen the medal before, just the ribbon. The ribbon was beautiful—mostly blue, with a narrow white stripe down either side and a red one down the middle. The medal was suspended from a bar across the bottom. It was a Maltese Cross, overlaid with a four-bladed propeller. It was a golden-bronze color. Although my initial impression when I opened the case was that it looked too much like the German Iron Cross, I was proud to get it, very proud. Now if I could just sneak in another milk run I could go home and show it off.

SEVENTEEN

NO EASY WAY

Sunday was wet and dreary, and I spent most of the afternoon at the club. I played a couple of games of Ping-Pong with Jack and he wiped me out, as usual, but I did manage to get fourteen points in the second game. I made some comment about this and Jack said, "Tell you what I'll do, Koger. I'll give you a handicap and play you another game."

He walked over and picked up a chair, a straight-backed, wooden chair used at the card tables. He set it down about three or four feet from the Ping-Pong table, sat down and leaned back, putting one heel up on the corner of the table. He grinned and said, "Serve!" About a dozen guys gathered around to watch Fromkin beat me while sitting down, which he did. I got in some good slams and some of them he couldn't return, particularly when I aimed for his foot, which was resting on the corner. He beat me twenty-one to sixteen.

I wasn't at all upset about this and, strange as it may sound, Jack wasn't at all a show-off. He was just in a much higher league than the rest of us, and this game wasn't intended to take me down a peg; it was an exhibition. Jack, the sleepy-eyed little guy with the shuffling walk, was simply uncanny with a Ping-Pong paddle. Some time ago, during a special night of some sort, he played Colonel Wilson a game. The Colonel was no slouch; he had won three or four games with good players when we ran Jack in on him. Jack showed our C.O. no mercy. Several times during the game the Colonel was defending himself against the bullet-like return, with no thought of trying to hit the ball. He just wanted to keep the ball from hitting him.

I stopped by the squadron office and checked the bulletin board. Nothing doing for tomorrow. I walked into the hut, wondering whether to write some letters or just sack out for awhile. A loud and familiar voice greeted me from the far end of the hut: "Koger, you old sonofabitch, ain't you through yet?!"

George Lester, the big farm-boy engineer from my first crew, walked up with a huge grin on his face. I stuck out my hand and yelled an astonished greeting, but he grabbed me in a bear hug and lifted me off the floor.

"Damn, George, I wondered if I'd see you again before I finished!"

"How many you got to go, anyhow?"

I stuck up one finger and said, "Not many!"

"George, dammit all, I thought several times about coming over to Oxford to see you, but I always chickened out and went to London instead."

He said, still grinning broadly, "Well, I'm all fixed up!" He pulled his pants legs up to the knees and turned around. The calves of his legs were horribly torn and discolored. The right leg was especially ugly, the muscles were torn out and sunken in as if they had atrophied. I said, "Boy, that flak played hell with your legs!"

George said, "Hell, there was a guy in the hospital that had worse than this in his *ass*! He laid on his stomach for two months."

"You just visiting, George? Where are they sending you?"

"Right here. I'm back in the 326th. They say I've got to finish my tour."

It had been four months ago that George was hit, and I remembered it being his seventh mission, or maybe his eighth. But I was surprised, and disappointed that they insisted on making him fly combat again. Despite his big grin and his apparent happiness to be back in the squadron, he'd been hurt in a B-17, *badly* hurt, and surely he wasn't looking forward to getting in one and going back to Germany. Maybe it just hadn't had time to sink in yet. Anyway, it was great to see him again.

George and I immediately became much closer than we were before he got hurt. We were friends then, but now he sort of latched onto me like I was his older brother. I was the only guy he knew. The rest of the crew was gone, and he hadn't had time to make many other friends before he got hurt.

Over the next few days we had many conversations. We drank a lot of beers together and talked about a lot of things. One thing was certain: he was scared to death of getting back into a B-17. He didn't exactly say this, although he came close, but I could tell that he had a morbid dread of starting the whole business over again. But whenever the conversation took that turn, he always got the broad grin going and said how proud he was of me getting through the whole tour, and getting my D.F.C., and all that. I'd remind him that I wasn't quite through yet, and he'd say, "Aw hell, Fred, one lousy mission, and they always give you a milk run on the last one, don't they?"

George and I generally checked the Alert List together. The Group flew on the twenty-first, but neither of us was on it. They went to Merseburg and got shot up, as usual. They didn't lose any planes, but took a lot of battle damage. The Division lost fourteen. We were on stand-down again for the next two days. I told George all about PFF bombing. There had been some of it when he was flying, but not like it was now. In fact, I didn't believe the Group had bombed visually for something like a month.

On the twenty-fourth the Group went back to Merseburg, and again I wasn't alerted. Neither was George. I decided to try for another pass to London, and asked George if he'd like to put in for one. He decided not to; I thought he wanted to get the first one in as soon as possible. The first one of Part Two of his tour, that is.

I left Wellingborough station on the morning train on the twenty-fifth. The weather was dreary and cold and I hadn't had a chance to call Barbara. I'd do that when I got to the Winston.

I called just before noon and got the duty room. The girl who answered the phone said she knew me; she was one of the ones I'd met the day I got chewed out by the Major. She said she'd have Barbara call me, and I gave her the phone number.

I decided to stick around the hotel and wait for the call, and went up to l'Auberge de France. Kay wasn't there, but my friend the "maitress d'" was, and I took my usual table by the window, alongside the grand piano. I sipped cups of tea and looked down on Jermyn Street in the rain, thinking about England, and flying, and the Winston, and Barbara, and how long ago my first mission seemed, and how soon it would all be over. I had a feeling in my guts that this would be the last time I'd see London. I was reminiscing, half-hypnotized when the lady with the pince-nez said I had a telephone call.

Barbara sounded happy to hear my voice, and the first thing she asked was whether I was finished flying. I said, "Not quite. Tell you all about it when I see you."

"I think there's a train at two, so I shall see you about two-thirty-ish," she said.

"I'll be at Victoria."

We didn't do much during the afternoon, just walked around Soho mostly. She hadn't noticed my D.F.C. and I hadn't mentioned it. I was pretty full of myself and made no bones about my eagerness to get the last mission over and get back to Texas. She said she was happy for me, and seemed to mean it.

Early in the evening I suggested we give the Universelle Brasserie a whirl, but she didn't care for the place. We had dinner at a large corner pub with leaded glass windows and lots of oak booths. During dinner I decided to impress Barbara, the unimpressible, with my new D.F.C. I mentioned it casually and pointed out the ribbon. She said, "That's marvelous. What did you do to get it?"

That's when I made my mistake. I tried to look modest and said something like, "Aw shucks, I'd rather not go into it."

She smiled, looked me right in the eyes, and said, "Isn't the D.F.C. award a rather automatic thing when you finish your ops?"

I grinned and said, "Shot down again! Can't put anything over on you, can I?"

After dinner we walked along Piccadilly toward Leicester Square, stopping occasionally in front of a theatre or cinema, but neither of us was interested in a movie. It was now dark—pitch dark, with no moon to give London that ethereal look. Finally I said, "How about going back to that little bar we found last time, the Salted Almond, I think it was."

She seemed to like the idea. I knew approximately where it was. She knew exactly.

We found a little booth and ordered drinks. I was in a happy-go-lucky mood, but Barbara wasn't as full of fun as usual. I had several times in the past insisted that I was going to take her back to Texas. She always laughed and said that was ridiculous—as it was. It was just a line, and she knew it.

I said it again tonight and got a different response. "Well, do you think you're gonna like Texas?"

She sounded very serious when she answered, "This business of Americans marrying English girls—it's not really sensible, you know. You'll marry a nice American girl and I'll find a nice English boy—"

I didn't say anything for awhile. Damn, I thought, I wasn't proposing! That was just my usual banter! Barbara was sitting quietly, looking down at the table, turning her glass between her forefingers. It was my turn to say something, and I didn't know what to say.

Our conversation got started again, and in a few minutes it was like it had never happened. She kidded me about my D.F.C. and accused me of acting like a movie hero. I kidded her about not having any more buzz bombs to shoot at.

By the time we got to Victoria Station we were acting normally, and I offered to ride with her to Dulwich. She insisted I shouldn't and this time I didn't argue. I told her I'd phone when I finished my last mission.

When I got back to the hut late on the twenty-sixth I found out that the Group had been out today. George still hadn't flown, but Jack and the other guys had, and they were just getting back to the hut. They had been to Misburg, another big oil refinery. The name was only vaguely familiar to me; I had heard a guy make a remark in the combat mess after one of the Merseburg missions, and it stuck in my mind. He'd said, "Well, I been to Magdeburg, and Misburg, and Merseburg, and I almost got my ass shot off at all of them, so I ain't going no place that starts with an 'M' and ends in 'burg.'"

From talking to some of the people that flew it didn't sound like Misburg was as bad as Merseburg. But it wasn't a milk run either. Battle damage was extremely heavy, and I heard that Misburg was Number Two on the Target Priority List. That surprised me; we had been concentrating on Merseburg and nobody had said anything at all about Misburg. Well, I thought, maybe we're through with it after today.

The next two days the Group went on stand-down again. Surely I wasn't going to drag this tour out into December. It had been almost two weeks since the Aachen raid, and I was getting really itchy to finish it. There was a Mission Alert for the twenty-ninth and my name wasn't on it. George was with me when we checked the board, and he wasn't alerted, either. He seemed as disappointed as I was. I wanted to finish and he wanted to get started again. I said to George as we walked back to the hut, "Well, they're probably going to Merseburg tomorrow and they wouldn't do that to me on my last mission."

The Group went back to Misburg without me on the twenty-ninth and bombed PFF, as usual. For some reason the flak was only moderate at most, and there was relatively light damage to the airplanes. It would have been a good one to finish with, I thought. But maybe they were waiting for a real milk run for my finale.

I was finally alerted to fly on the last day of November. So was George. We talked about it in a casual way, but he was full of anticipation, or probably something more like dread, while I was jittery as hell. We discussed the probable targets and came up with answers that neither one of us like. Every mission since the middle of November had been *oil*; the Group had only flown four times, once to Merseburg and three times to Misburg.

Finally George said, "Well I don't have any choice tomorrow, but you do."

"What do you mean, *choice?*"

"You've got a choice on your last mission. You can pass and wait for the next time."

I'd heard that too, but I wasn't sure whether it was true or just another latrine rumor. I had a lot of trouble sleeping, and when the lights came on I was wide awake in a split second. I looked at my watch and it was just after two-thirty. That's an awfully early wake up for a milk run.

George and I parted company after breakfast. He headed for gunners' briefing and I walked warily into the main briefing room. My "lucky" area on the left had plenty of seats, and I took one about halfway down the room, on the left aisle. I lit a cigarette, as I always did, and looked around the room. It was about half full, and people were coming in steadily. I had sat in the exact spot, or close to it, so many times before. But never had I been as nervous as I was this morning. Never.

My row filled up and somebody sat down next to me. I don't know whether he was a navigator or a bombardier or what. Colonel Wilson walked in and proceded toward the front of the room, accompanied by his retinue of officers and a loud "Ten-shun!" Two-hundred pairs of feet scuffled on the concrete and the chairs squeaked as we stood up. The Colonel smiled his warm, sincere smile and said, "At ease," and then, "Good morning!"

When the curtain was pulled back and the big map exposed it took me a few seconds to comprehend where the red string went. It stretched far into east Germany, and the bends in the string looked more or less familiar to me. I still hadn't decided for sure what the target was—I couldn't read the map from thirty feet away—until the voice from the front said, "Today we will attack the I. G. Farben Industrie synthetic oil refinery complex at Merseburg."

The nervousness, the queasy feeling in my stomach, disappeared, drained away in a second or two, to be replaced by a numb feeling, as if all hope had departed along with the nervousness.

I always listened carefully at briefing, sometimes even enjoyed it, since those first two or three missions when I felt I was just being carried along helplessly. Today I had that same feeling. I heard the voices of the weather guys giving the briefing as if they were far away, catching only an occasional phrase: "cloud cover in the target area should be no more than four-tenths—bombing should be visual— "The I.P. is here, at Eisleben—we expect to encounter intense flak over the target."

At the beginning of the briefing I made up my mind that I was going to exercise my option to pass on this one. I wondered if I really had such an option; I thought so. It was my last mission. But I had never heard of anybody passing on their last mission. I never saw anybody do it. I wondered how to go about it. Should I stand up and raise my hand? Jesus, I couldn't do *that*!

Soon the briefing was over and I was shuffling out with the other bombardiers. I thought about asking one of them if there really was an option on your last mission. But if I didn't know for sure, neither would they. I doubt if any of them had as many missions as I had, so if anybody knew for sure, I should. And I didn't.

Then I was in the equipment room, drawing my gear and putting on the stuff I needed to go to war. I knew I was going. I didn't know when, or whether I made the decision to go. I just went.

The hardstand was dark when I got off the truck and walked toward the airplane. There were a couple of guys moving around, so I wasn't the first one here. I shoved my gear through the nose hatch and pulled myself in after it, thinking that this was probably the last time I would have to perform this semi-acrobatic feat.

I looked out of the nose and it seemed that everybody was here now. I'd heard some others in the back of the plane from time to time. I decided I might as well join them and help pull the props through. I got my escape kit from the copilot and he said, "Hell of a place to go on your last mission, Koger."

"If I could go someplace else, I sure as hell would!" I told him.

The rest of the guys on the crew had about a dozen missions yet to fly—some more, some less. I was the only one finishing today. In this airplane, anyway. By the time we were ready to climb in for good almost every one of the guys had said something to me about my last mission. Nobody said "Good Luck." I was glad they didn't; after all, we were all going in the same airplane.

We left the runway at 0932. Usually I didn't check the exact time, but for some reason I glanced to my left and read the time on my panel clock while I pulled up on the seat to try to help get the damn B-17 into the air. I always strained, tugging at the seat, during takeoff.

Forming up was the usual circling, climbing, circling, climbing as one by one the B-17s with the big white "B" in the black triangle found each other. I watched the planes for a while, then the ground. The planes were still bright and silver and beautiful in the morning sunlight. The ground was different, but I hadn't really noticed it until now. I hadn't really *seen* it from the air for the last couple of months, it seemed. It was no longer shades of lush green, but tan and brown, separated by green hedgerows and dotted here and there with patches of woods. Winter had almost come to England. Tomorrow it would be December.

We crossed over the English coast at Felixstowe, and after a few minutes I called the flight deck and asked the pilot if it was OK to arm the bombs. Of course it was OK to arm the bombs, so I went back into the bomb bay and returned to the nose with my pockets stuffed with tags and cotter pins.

We were on oxygen and still climbing when the navigator called out on the intercom, "Crossing the coastline. Ostend just ahead."

I called for an oxygen check at about the time we approached the German border. Arnhem was somewhere down below, and I wondered how those British airborne troops who lived through that battle were doing now—probably in prison camps somewhere in Germany.

By the time we got to the I.P. my gut was doing flip-flops. I had wanted to get into my flak suit half an hour ago, but I waited until Shorty suggested it just before the I.P. I scanned the area to our right, about two o'clock, and didn't see the black cloud, so we must be first over the target today.

I hadn't been able to relax since I climbed into the airplane. I was aware of every sound, every change in prop pitch, every little increase or decrease in engine power. I was acutely aware of things that should have been so routine to me by now. But today wasn't a routine day. Again and again I tried to tell myself that this was just another mission, just like the other thirty-four, but I couldn't convince myself. Things went through my mind that had never occurred to me before. What if we lost an engine and had to abort? Then I'd have to go through this all over again, and I wasn't sure that my nerves would stand it.

Shortly after we turned on the I.P. the flak started. It was heavy and it was close, and the puffs multiplied until we were surrounded by them. Once again there was no place to go but straight ahead, and that was where it was worst. Goggles down over the mask, eyes fixed on the lead plane, I tried not to look at the flak. It would only be ten more minutes or so. It occurred to me that I had been meaning to time a bomb run and now it was too late. And it was the least important thing I had to worry about.

We were probably in the target area for fifteen minutes. It was, very simply, the longest fifteen minutes of my life!

"Seventeen going down!" It was the waist gunner's voice, I think.

Somebody said, "Where. Who?"

"High element number one."

I looked away from the lead plane for a few seconds and stared back over our left wing. The crippled B-17 was a few yards under his formation companions, nose up a little, faltering. Then he slid slowly downward, not in a dive, but more like a glide. He was falling behind very rapidly, and banking slightly to the right. In just a few seconds he was out of my sight, and my eyes snapped back to focus again on the lead plane.

"There's one chute, and another one." That was definitely the tail gunner's voice. "There's one; that's three out!"

"Is he on fire?"

"Smoking. White smoke. I don't see any fire—Goddamn, he blew up!"

"Who was it? Does anybody know?"

"Smith I think."

There were two Smiths in the squadron, two that were first pilots. One of them was Arthur M., the other one I couldn't remember by his first name. A. M. was the tall, gangly one.

Somebody asked, "How many you think got out?"

"I don't know," said the tail gunner. "At least three. It looked like the pilot was trying to keep the nose up so they could jump. He was having trouble. The plane kept wanting to go into a dive."

We were in a steep right bank and I was still looking back as far around as I could, trying to see some sight of the doomed Fort, when I realized we were not getting any more flak. All four engines were still running, and I was still alive. I was finished! It didn't sink in right away. It had been a while since we'd had an oxygen check, so I called for one.

The pilot got on the intercom and notified us that it was A. M. Smith flying that position. I asked, "Wasn't he almost through with his tour?"

"Yeah, I think so. And you *are* through, Koger, if I can get this thing back to Podington."

"Well, you can't say I finished up on a milk run."

I spent the next hour munching my candy bars, peering at the ground and locating our position on the map, watching the other B-17s in the formation gently rising and falling alongside us, and developing a splitting headache. I decided it must be a migraine. I didn't have migraine headaches, that I knew of, but I had heard people talk about them, and this felt like what they had described. It was funny, I thought, this was the first headache I'd had since I started flying—except for the hangover kind, and this was different. I couldn't figure out what caused it. It wasn't tension. Maybe it was relief from tension. Maybe I could get a couple of A.P.C. pills in the Interrogation hut.

Two hours later we approached the coast of Belgium, and the headache was gone—completely gone. I was beginning to feel an exhilaration unlike anything I'd ever felt before. I wanted to jump up and down, and yell, and laugh, and celebrate. I'm through, dammit, through! I won't have to sweat out whether my name's on the Alert List, or get up at two-thirty in the morning and wonder where we're going, or sit half-paralyzed and watch the flak, or jump with fear when I hear a distant "pop," or see a burning B-17 hanging upside down right beside me. I was through!

I took off my oxygen mask at 13,000, and when we were well over the Channel I got up and crawled back through the hatch under the flight deck. The engineer grinned and stuck out his hand. I gave it a firm grip and he yelled, "How does it feel?" The pilot and copilot turned around, and the pilot grinned and gave me a thumbs up.

I tiptoed along the catwalk through the bomb bay and opened the radio room door. Bill nodded and waved a gloved right hand in a Kansas-style "howdy." I started to light up a Lucky, but Bill was busy, and besides, he was a pipe smoker. So I walked into the waist and got another handshake and sat down to have a cigarette with Martin. After a few puffs I ground it out and said I'd better get back up front. I wanted to be in the nose. It was where I was comfortable and secure. The only reason I had taken the trip through the airplane was that I was so keyed up I just couldn't sit still.

When I settled back in my seat I could barely make out the English coast through the broken clouds. I leaned forward and watched the coastline slide beneath us. England looked cold and gray. And it looked wonderful.

When our tires squealed on the runway at Podington I was in my usual position, right up front against the Plexiglas, looking back at the left gear to see the big tire smoke and start rolling. Sometime during the time it took to taxi to our hardstand I glanced at the clock on my panel. It was five-thirty.

Interrogation just about did me in. Guys kept coming by and pouring part of their Scotch into my glass. This was the accepted but unofficial custom for acknowledging that I'd finished my tour. When it was over I walked outside, found my bicycle, and discovered I couldn't make it go in a straight line. Finally I got off and just pushed it along, grateful for something to lean on. By the time I got to the hut I was feeling better. The first person I ran into was George. He yelled, "Where were you at Interrogation? I wanted to give you some of my booze!"

"I didn't need it, George. How the hell did you make out today?"

He hadn't made out too well. They got their plane shot up pretty badly, and came back with one engine out. When they landed the right landing gear caught fire from leaking hydraulic fluid, and George jumped out while the plane was still rolling and beat out the fire with his leather helmet. I tried to find out how his nerves were, and how he was feeling about starting his tour again, but all he wanted to do was laugh and congratulate me on being finished.

Merseburg was one hell of a way for George to start flying again, and one hell of a way for me to finish. The First Division had put up 400 B-17s, of which eleven were shot down and 287 damaged. The staff sergeant gunners were still hitting about three out of four.

The Ninety-second didn't fly for the next three days. After that I didn't know when or where they flew, because I wasn't there any longer.

EIGHTEEN

AFTER THE BATTLE

Leighton asked over his left shoulder, "Next stop Podington?"

"You bet," I answered.

We passed the old number one hangar and the road turned a bit to the left. I peered through the back window of the taxi at the control tower until it was out of sight behind a little stand of trees.

Leighton turned again and said, "This old road must look very familiar to you, eh?"

"Not at all, Leighton. I don't think I was in Podington more than two or three times."

He was surprised, and so was Sara. I explained that Podington was the official location of the Ninety-second Bomb Group, but it didn't offer the facilities we were looking for. "You'll see what I mean when we get there," I said.

After half a dozen turns in the winding little lane, and about that many minutes later, we were in the main street of the village.

Sara gave a little gasp, and said, "What a beautiful place! Look at the thatch roofs and the old church. It's gorgeous!"

We got out of the taxi and I took the lens cap off the Pentax while Sara did a three-sixty, taking in the beauty of the picturesque little village. She couldn't believe that I hadn't spent more time here. I said, "You've got to remember, honey, that we weren't looking for thatched roofs and cobblestone streets. We were looking for pubs and girls and movie theaters—the necessities of life!"

About the only thing I recognized in Podington was the old church spire, and actually I had seen it mostly from the air, from the nose of a B-17. We had always sighted in on it to be sure we were at the right airfield. Every village in England had a church spire, and to the casual looker they were all alike. But they aren't. We could tell the difference between our church spire and the ones at Thurleigh or Chelveston or Kimbolton, all of them within a few miles of each other.

We spent perhaps thirty minutes and a roll of film in Podington, then

I suggested we head for Rushden. I asked Leighton to let us off in the middle of town and meet us there again at four o'clock to drive us to the station at Wellingborough. He smiled and said, "Right. Meet you here at four. Have a lovely afternoon!"

I asked Sara if she was about ready for a break and a cold Schweppes lemonade, and she said absolutely. It was *past* time to take a breather.

"Okay, let's go introduce you to the Waggon and Horses, my favorite pub."

She suggested I'd better ask for directions, but I said, "I don't think so." We walked along the winding street past the huge old church on the left and I said, "If it's still here after forty years, it's just around the next bend to the right."

The Waggon and Horses was right where it was supposed to be, and I had walked to it as unerringly as if I'd been there forty minutes ago instead of forty years. It looked exactly as I remembered it. But not on the inside—to my dismay, the old oak and mahogany and brass and the dim lighting had been "modernized." Now it was knotty pine walls and bright fluorescent lighting, and they had knocked down a wall or two to make it more open and airy. The irony of it was that I'd seen people back home spend tens of thousands of dollars to try to create the atmosphere that the Waggon and Horses used to have.

Sara and I stood at the bar and sipped our drinks and chatted with the barman and the few customers. They were delighted to find out that I had come back after so many years, and raised their glasses to us. I stood a round for the house and ordered two shepherd's pies. The barman smiled and said, "Would you like fresh eggs on top? Bet you couldn't 'ave that in 1944!"

I laughed and said, "You're right, we couldn't. And yes, we would like it that way!"

Rushden really hadn't changed too much. It was a bit larger now, and the shops didn't need a coat of paint, but the narrow winding streets were the same and the two-hundred-year-old church was still the focal point of the town. The cinema was long gone, displaced by the telly. And the shop where I bought my bicycle was now an office of some kind.

But Rushden didn't have the same feeling to me. The difference was that there was no war going on. There was no air base just down the road, with Americans shattering the early morning quiet with the roar of B-17s taking off to go drop bombs or get shot down over Germany. There was no rationing, no shortage of anything, no absence of automobiles. The streets weren't filled with young men in olive-drab uniforms who had a compulsion to have fun, as much fun as possible, as quickly as possible. There were no young men in a hurry to drink mild-and-bitter and play darts and go to the cinema and get a date with a local girl. Most of the people we met could scarcely remember that time. But some could.

Sara and I talked for the better part of an hour with a lovely lady who owned a dress shop just off the main street. She was born in Rushden, and was in her twenties when the town was invaded by the American flyboys. She smiled when she talked about the Liberty Run trucks and the Americans wrecking their bikes after they'd had too much to drink and our casual approach to combat flying.

"We were more than casual," I commented. "We were a cocky bunch of pains in the neck. We overran the town and tried to inflict our customs on you folks!"

She smiled and shook her head. "Oh no. No, not at all. You were just young men doing a dangerous thing, and I remember you all with fondness."

The English, it appears, took things like wars and Americans in stride.

The London train from Wellingborough still stops at Bedford and Luton. The little train station at Wellingborough was exactly the same red brick building with the ornate Victorian ironwork, except that I don't remember flower boxes in the windows in 1944. But maybe there were. In 1944 I wasn't taking time to stop and smell the roses. I was in a hurry all the time, it seems.

Sara and I took the evening train from Wellingborough and talked most of the way to London. One of her comments struck me as being odd, or at least unexpected. She said, "I'd like to meet Barbara. Do you suppose you could find out where she lives?"

"Good Lord, honey, after *forty years*? I wouldn't know where to start looking!"

She said that she and Leighton had talked at length while I was off by myself, prowling around the old air base. She told him about Barbara and he'd asked if I corresponded with her after I left England. She wasn't sure.

The fact is, I hadn't. It's not that I didn't intend to, but just the way things worked out. I tried to explain how things changed so suddenly when I finished my tour. It was difficult to understand, but my fondness for Barbara, and for London, were always secondary. In 1944 the center of my world was Podington—the Ninety-second Group. Everything else was just a temporary diversion. My sole purpose was to fly missions. Time was reckoned not by weeks or months, but by how many missions I'd flown. My stay in England wasn't for a period of months, but a set number of combat missions.

And on that last day of November, 1944, my war was finished. My world was no longer made up of early-morning briefings, bombers, flak, fear, trips to London. Suddenly I didn't have to do that any more, and the transition to normal, non-combat life was enormous. My entire perspective changed. *Everything* changed.

On reflection, the way that I dropped Barbara like a hot potato seemed very callous. I had dropped everything that had been important to me when I finished my combat tour, including my brief but fondly remembered "wartime romance."

During the ensuing days I showed Sara my favorite city . . . in depth. I wasn't sure whether she'd like London as much as I did, but I needn't have worried. She loved it. Sara became an unashamed Anglophile overnight, just as I had forty years ago. I took her to the Universelle Brasserie, which isn't called that anymore. But it was still there, under the Criterion, and we had a drink there.

The old Winston Hotel was now a branch bank, but the theater-like marquee was still out front. And we spent many pleasant hours in the mezzanine tearoom at Simpson's Piccadilly looking down on Jermyn Street. It was the same view I had when I sat at the window next to the grand piano in l'Auberge de France, just a block further down the street. And I didn't go out at night looking for the Piccadilly Commandos, although I suspect they may still be in operation—not the same ones, one hopes, but their younger replacements.

The most interesting phenomena about our two weeks in London took me completely by surprise. I still don't completely understand the reason for it. Much of the time in London I wore a lapel pin, about the size of a dime, a replica of the Eighth Air Force patch—the Winged Eight. I did this just for sentimental reasons, and figured nobody would pay any attention to it or, for that matter, know what it was.

But people did. Hardly a day went by that somebody didn't look more closely at the pin and say, "Pardon me, but isn't that an Eighth Air Force badge?" Then a conversation would ensue, with questions about where I was based, what kind of plane I flew, how many "ops" I did, and always the key question, "Tell me, did you chaps really fly all your operations in daylight?" It was as if they were saving that question until they got to know me a little better, and the way they asked sounded as if they wanted to add, "You really *didn't*, did you?"

The thing that amazed me was the interest in us after forty years. Another fact that qualified as amazing was that, in most cases, the people were too young to have participated in the war. Most were ex-RAF, some were current RAF, some were just aviation buffs. But all of them were very familiar with the Eighth and very eager to talk with someone who actually flew with that mighty force.

One fellow who stopped me was an American, about my age. Sara and I were browsing the antique shops along Kensington Church Street when this man tapped me on the shoulder and said, "Excuse me." I turned around and he introduced himself and said he'd noticed my pin in the last shop we'd browsed, and he wanted to buy it! He explained that he was retired and had moved from New Jersey to London a couple of years ago. He was a B-24 Navigator in 1944 and he had to have one of these pins. I declined his offer to buy it and told him where I'd found it back in the States.

We swapped stories for a while and, less than an hour later, ducked under an awning to get out of a sudden rain shower, where we were joined shortly by a well-dressed Londoner. He was pinstriped and hair-styled and carrying a Harrod's shopping bag. I would guess he was about forty, maybe forty-five. He spotted the pin and immediately started questioning me about my experiences with the Eighth. He had served in the RAF for six years and was currently a reserve pilot. He had an intense interest in the Eighth Air Force, and wound up inviting us to tea in his flat, which was "just up at the top of Church Street." We declined with thanks.

Those encounters came as a great surprise to me. Perhaps the fact that we were based in England accounts for the interest. Perhaps some of these people were kids living near one of our bases in 1943 and 1944. Whatever the reason, it was nice that people recognized the emblem. And even nicer to be treated almost like a celebrity.

I believe the Eighth Air Force still exists, somewhere in the Training Command. Maybe it's merged with a bunch of other numbered units, I'm not really sure. But once upon a time it was the *Mighty Eighth*, and it was famous.

In some places, to some people, it still is.